LEGENDS AND LORE C

PARANORMAL
PROVINCETOWN

Sam
Baltrusis

Schiffer Publishing Ltd

4880 Lower Valley Road • Atglen, PA 19310

Library Control Number: 2016939418

Designed by RoS
Cover design by Matt Goodman
Type set in Verlag/Chronicle Text G1
ISBN: 978-0-7643-5153-2
Printed in the United States of America

Published by Schiffer Publishing, Ltd.
4880 Lower Valley Road
Atglen, PA 19310
Phone: (610) 593-1777; Fax: (610) 593-2002
E-mail: Info@schifferbooks.com
Web: www.schifferbooks.com

For our complete selection of fine books on this and related subjects, please visit our website at www.schifferbooks.com. You may also write for a free catalog.

Schiffer Publishing's titles are available at special discounts for bulk purchases for sales promotions or premiums. Special editions, including personalized covers, corporate imprints, and excerpts, can be created in large quantities for special needs. For more information, contact the publisher.

We are always looking for people to write books on new and related subjects. If you have an idea for a book, please contact us at proposals@schifferbooks.com.

TO THE LADY OF THE DUNES

Historic aerial view of Provincetown Harbor and MacMillan Wharf. Former police chief Jeff Jaran estimated that Provincetown has become the second largest Halloween gathering in Massachusetts right behind Salem. *Courtesy Boston Public Library, Print Department.*

CONTENTS

ACKNOWLEDGMENTS

After writing *Paranormal Provincetown*, my internal batteries are recharged and I'm grateful to have fallen back in love with the town that has had such a huge impact on my creative life. I had to trudge through Provincetown's darker side to ultimately see its beauty. Back in 2009, I had what is known as a "spiritual awakening" while swimming in the Atlantic Ocean. I feel so in touch with Provincetown's energy—both the good and bad. There's an underlying spirit of magic there. It's good magic and the beauty is in the small things...like watching the sun shimmer on the rocks as you walk with your friend along the shore of Herring Cove. Thanks to my spirit squad from Boston Haunts and Cambridge Haunts, including Nick Cox, and Hank Fay, for helping me rouse the dead and give a voice to those long departed. The Haunted Ptown ghost tour I co-produced with my friend Jeffrey Doucette helped shape the tone and lore featured in *Paranormal Provincetown*. Also, I wrote a large feature for *Boston Spirit* magazine on Provincetown's haunted hotspots in 2012, and the heart of this book stems from the cover story featuring Adam Berry formerly of Syfy's *Ghost Hunters*. Major thanks to the handful of paranormal investigators and researchers who helped make *Paranormal Provincetown* a reality, including Adam Berry; Michael Baker from Para-Boston; authors Sandra Lee, Joni Mayhan, and Peter Muise; former Cambridge Haunts guide Ashley Shakespeare; and Jeffrey Doucette, a veteran tour guide who appeared in my first book, *Ghosts of Boston: Haunts of the Hub*. I would like to give my friend and copy editor Andrew Warburton a supernatural slap on the back. He helped me uncover some of the skeletal secrets featured in this monstrous project. Thanks to my mother, Deborah Hughes Dutcher, for being there when I needed her most and my friends for their continued support. I would also like to thank Dinah Roseberry from Schiffer Publishing for her help during the process of putting this book together. Special thanks to H. P. Lovecraft for his creative use of *Arkham*-inspired phrases like "vaporous corpse-light, yellow and diseased" and Stephen King for terrifying me as a kid with the horror classic, *The Shining*.

Opposite:
Next stop? Provincetown. Located at the extreme tip of Cape Cod, Ptown's year-round population averages a few thousand and swells to 60,000 during the summer. The dramatic increase during the warmer months doesn't include its ghostly inhabitants. *Photo by Sam Baltrusis.*

INTRODUCTION

On All Hallow's Eve, Provincetown's Commercial Street was abuzz with both the living...and the dead. I was on a walking tour with ghost host Jeffrey Doucette, a former colleague at Haunted Boston and co-founder of Haunted Ptown, a tour I helped produce. As Doucette and I crept through the dark alleys of the town, revelers paraded up and down the main drag.

"The weather has been a horror show," said Doucette, a veteran tour guide known for his over-the-top theatrics and spine-tingling delivery. He was dressed in a tuxedo, holding a lantern and sporting a skull face paint job. "Look at 'em," he said with a smile. "The freaks are out tonight." He pointed at the crews of scantily clad trick-or-treaters showing off their costumes.

Compared to Salem on Halloween, Provincetown's fearsome phantoms constructed the most elaborate and creative costumes I've ever seen.

A vampiric-looking man was standing in front of Whaler's Wharf with pointy ears and fangs, showing off his "Cape Cod Casket Co." coffin. He looked like an adult version of Eddie Munster. He playfully hissed and posed for a picture. A flock of fractured fairytale fairies were wearing green tutus and granting make-believe wishes with magic wands.

There was one figure sitting on a bench dressed like a "bat boy." He was hiding in the shadows as passersby admired his expertly crafted costume. Looking closely, his eyes were red and the fur covering his face looked extremely authentic. I was genuinely creeped out.

"You've seen the movie *Jeepers Creepers*, right?" mused Doucette. "Well, Provincetown has its own boogieman. He's known as the Black Flash."

According to legend, a grim reaper-type beast was known to snatch children away. The cryptid made national headlines. When the phantom of Provincetown was first reported in the 1930s, some locals were suspicious that the creature had arrived around Halloween.

Surely it was just a prank, right? Not according to reports.

Dressed in a black cape, the monster appeared to have bat wings and was known to suddenly drop into a visitor's path from a tree or rooftop. "He was all black with eyes like balls of flame," claimed one man in a 1930s-era newspaper account. "And he was big, maybe eight feet tall. He made a sound, a loud buzzing sound, like a June bug on a hot day, only louder."

One boy claimed that "it jumped out" at him from nowhere "and spit blue flames" in his face. Alleged sightings of the Black Flash continued for a decade. One townie, who found his dog barking at the demon, claimed he shot it. However, he said that the Flash dodged his bullets and continued to laugh maniacally. The creature then leaped over the man's backyard fence.

The Black Flash made its last appearance in the mid-1940s when it supposedly chased a family home. As they gathered inside, one of the school-aged children doused the creature with a bucket of water—similar to what Dorothy did to the Wicked Witch in *The Wizard of Oz*. It's not been seen since.

Or has it?

"He's known to come out on Halloween," continued Doucette. "But I think it's just an old legend to keep the kiddies from staying out too late."

After the Haunted Ptown tour, I returned to the bench where I spotted the furry cryptid earlier. He was gone. What was odd about the costume is that its head was way too small compared to the rest of its body. And his perfectly crafted bat wings. Man, they were so authentic. And, like in Doucette's story, his eyes were red, "like balls of flame."

I walked up and down Commercial Street looking for the *Mothman Prophecies* look-a-like. No luck. Like the legend, he was gone in a flash.

As the witching hour approached, I headed to Provincetown's cemetery. Over the years, I've spent afternoons at the Winthrop Street graveyard looking at the historic headstones. At the time, I was working on an investigative piece for a magazine about the infamous unsolved murder

Provincetown has four cemeteries. Its oldest is located off Winslow Street behind the fire station on Shank Painter Road. *Photo by Sam Baltrusis.*

of the Lady of the Dunes. For some reason, I couldn't find her grave marker at the nearby St. Peter's Cemetery.

The cold case I was writing about has haunted Provincetown for more than four decades. The Lady of the Dunes was found in a deserted service road hidden in the Race Point Dunes. On July 26, 1976, a teenage girl who was walking her dog discovered the naked, decomposing body of a woman in her twenties or early thirties. The woman was lying face down and blue jeans (which were Wrangler) were found at the scene and placed under her head. A green towel was also found at the scene. She had long auburn or reddish hair in a ponytail and she was approximately 5-foot-6 inches tall. She had an athletic build.

The Lady of the Dunes, as she has been nicknamed, had extensive dental work on her teeth, worth thousands of dollars. The killer had removed several of those teeth—a practice that James "Whitey" Bulger and his cronies were known for. Her hands had also been removed and she was nearly decapitated and had received massive trauma to the side of her skull. Police believe she was also sexually assaulted. Her body has been exhumed twice, in 1980 and 2000, so forensic testing could be performed. No luck.

However, a new lead suggested the Lady of the Dunes was tied to notorious Winter Hill Gang leader, James "Whitey" Bulger. In fact, Bulger (who had a past as a gay-for-pay male hustler) was a regular at the popular gay hangout, The Crown & Anchor, and had recently been linked to a woman with a similar description as the Lady of the Dunes. There was also a size 10 shoe imprint found at the scene, the same shoe size as Whitey Bulger, and a green towel or blanket believed to be from the Crown & Anchor.

Did Whitey do it? Evidence suggested he should have been a person of interest. As we've seen with this notorious cold case, beautiful places aren't immune to brutal crimes.

Armed with a flashlight, I found the Lady of the Dunes' grave marker. The headstone in Provincetown's St. Peter's Cemetery is merely labeled "unidentified female." As I approached, I heard the sound of scampering feet and spotted a tiny figure dart by as I gasped for air. I was terrified.

At first, I thought it was a cat. And then, based on my past experiences with the paranormal, I assumed it was a cemetery-bound spirit. Or, as I joked to myself based on experiences with my third book *Ghosts of Salem: Haunts of the Witch City*, it could have been a ghost cat.

I lifted my flashlight and saw two eyes peering back at me. It was a red fox. We both looked at each other as I shivered in the beauty and the madness of the moment.

If you believe in Native American shamanism, the fox is a spirit animal and an omen of sorts. According to Native superstition, it's a warning of "dark magic" involved in an upcoming project.

The Pilgrims first set foot on Cape Cod on November 21, 1620, and spent five weeks exploring the Outer Cape before signing the Mayflower Compact and heading to Plymouth. *Photo by Sam Baltrusis.*

I quickly darted out of the cemetery and headed back to my hotel. Of course, it's no surprise that I was put into the one room at the Provincetown Inn that is allegedly haunted. I have stayed in this *The Shining*-esque hotel with killer views of the harbor many times since I moved back to Boston in 2007. I never scored the so-called haunted room, which is No. 23, until Halloween.

It was after midnight and, of course, I couldn't sleep a wink.

The wing I was staying in was usually off limits, unless the place is at max capacity or it's during the winter. My room was facing the harbor and I spent most of the evening transfixed by the view of the Pilgrim Monument and the water.

Unfortunately, I had no ghostly encounters at the Provincetown Inn that night.

However, I have seen what appeared to be an inexplicable shadow glide down the hallway one New Year's Eve night a few years ago. I've also stayed at most of the allegedly haunted hotels scattered throughout Provincetown.

My first face-to-face haunted encounter in Provincetown was at Revere Guest House on Court Street. Staying in Room 8 on the top level, I watched in awe as the doorknob turned and I saw what looked like a nineteenth-century fisherman pass through the small hallway from neighboring Room 7. During a second visit, I heard what sounded like a single marble roll down the hall.

According to the owner, Gary Palochko, a sea captain named Jackson Rogers from the Azores owned the house in the 1860s and, during renovations in 2004, the B&B owner uncovered a nineteenth-century map. When I mentioned my spirited encounter, Palochko shrugged and said ghosts "scare customers away." However, he said that inexplicable noises heard by previous guests in Room 8 stopped once he found the map and other hidden treasures from the 1860s.

Based on historical research, there were three kids—Jennie, Manuel, and Joseph—in the Rogers family, as well as the fisherman's wife, Mary. Based on my experience and other reports, the paranormal activity sounded like a residual haunting or a non-intelligent, videotaped replay of past events.

What about the weird sound I heard in the hall? The Revere Guest House owner sheepishly told me that he also uncovered an antique marble buried within the walls.

Also, in 2007, I spent the night at what turned out to be Provincetown's murder house. I was on assignment for a magazine and had booked a weekend at the Victoria House on Standish Street. I was put into Room 4 and spent the night under my covers because I heard what sounded like muted cries or a whimper coming from a boarded-up closet. The following

The 252-feet-tall Pilgrim Monument is the tallest all-granite structure in the United States and was officially unveiled on August 5, 1910. *Photo by Sam Baltrusis.*

morning, I asked to be moved out of the spooky room. I intuitively knew something horrible had happened there.

Years later I found out that the Victoria House had a dark secret. Back in the 1960s, the B&B was a guest house and was home to serial killer Tony "Chop Chop" Costa. He was convicted in 1970 of two of the four murders of the young women he allegedly slaughtered, including Patricia H. Walsh and Mary Ann Wysocki. For a brief period, the house was pointed out to tourists as the site where the murderer lived. Costa met his victims there before luring them to his "secret garden" of marijuana and murdering and mutilating them in Truro.

According to the July 25, 1969 article in *Life* magazine penned by *Slaughterhouse-Five* author Kurt Vonnegut Jr., Costa's room at the Standish Street haunt was significant. "In his closet in the rooming house where he helped Patricia Walsh and Mary Ann Wysocki with their luggage, police found a coil of stained rope," Vonnegut wrote.

After a topsy-turvy Halloween night at the Provincetown Inn, I called a cab the following morning. The driver, who looked to be in her early thirties and who drove a black-and-white checkerboard car, asked why I was visiting.

"Research," I said. "I write historical-based ghost books."

She nodded and talked about her one close encounter with what she described as a shadow figure. "It was plain as day," recalled the cab driver. "I saw a black figure. It looked like a shadow and it passed right by me in the kitchen. My mom passed one month later. I will never forget that night."

"Were you scared?" I asked. She shook her head. "I don't believe in ghosts," she said with a laugh. The cabbie dropped me off at the bus station as I slowly gathered my belongings. "But I do think Ptown is haunted," she added as I slammed the door shut.

One of Provincetown's more notorious shipwrecks included the tourist boat S.S. *Romance*, which sank in September 1936 en route to Ptown. There were no casualties from the *Romance* tragedy. *Courtesy Boston Public Library, Print Department.*

÷ 14 ÷

CHAPTER 1

COMMERCIAL HAUNTS

P aranormal activity in Provincetown? Adam Berry, formerly from *Ghost Hunters* and a year-round resident, said that you can't throw a rock down Commercial Street, the town's main drag, without hitting a haunted hotspot. "You're looking at one of the oldest places on the Cape. Yes, it's haunted," mused Berry when *Paranormal Provincetown* asked him if the resort town is chock full of spirits... and we don't mean the kind that comes in a chilled Martini glass.

"Provincetown is where the Pilgrims first landed. It's where they set up shop. It has to be haunted," said Berry, who co-founded the Provincetown Paranormal Research Society (PPRS) with his partner Ben Griessmeyer in 2006. "If you think about all of the shipwrecks in Provincetown, Wellfleet, and Truro, there's got to be something here."

Griessmeyer echoed Berry's belief that Provincetown is a hotbed of paranormal activity. "The inspiration to develop the PPRS came purely from the amount of tales, legends, and ghost stories that had piled up since we first summered here in 2003," Griessmeyer explained. "Over the years we heard things about the old Lancy Mansion on Commercial Street and how it's haunted by an old woman [who died in the late 1800s] and due to the frozen ground couldn't be buried. Her son kept her propped up in an open window all winter long. Also, there are tales of the Martin House ghosts and also the Black Flash of Provincetown—a grim reaper-type beast that would snatch children away in the 1930s—that perked our interest in starting PPRS."

In fact, Berry and Griessmeyer took their passion for the paranormal to the altar. In August 2012, they tied the knot at one of the Outer

Since retiring from *Ghost Hunters*, Adam Berry continues to give paranormal-themed lectures with former on-air partner Amy Bruni. *Courtesy Adam Berry.*

Cape's most-haunted locales, Provincetown's town hall. "It used to be an old jail and the people who work there say that the offices downstairs are haunted," Berry said, adding that Town Hall's former jail once housed Marlon Brando, who spent the night in the drunk tank after playing bongos on the street. "I don't have proof, but people say that it's haunted. During construction, employees claimed that tools and ladders were moved and that you could hear disembodied voices, which makes sense because construction usually brings up activity."

Griessmeyer, who frequently travels with his husband to haunted locations scattered throughout the country, said his interest in the paranormal has been satiated thanks to Berry's work. "There are some perks that come along with being married to a paranormal investigator. As a young boy some of my favorite movies were of the *Ghostbusters* variety, and as an adult, it seems that my childhood wishes to ghost hunt have vicariously come to fruition," Griessmeyer emoted. "With Adam by my side, there will always be a treasure trove of *true* ghost stories to tell around a campfire, and I'll never really have to be afraid of the dark anymore because he knows how to handle a flashlight."

Griessmeyer said he's had a few close encounters of the paranormal kind while traveling with Berry. "Disembodied voices are pretty spooky

Historic photo of a Commercial Street storefront in the West End. *Courtesy Boston Public Library, Print Department.*

to me," Griessmeyer added. "I was at the Stanley Hotel with Adam, and while investigating on the fourth floor, we both heard a voice whispering right next to me. You could make out the consonants and everything. Gave me the chills!"

When it comes to confronting ghosts, Berry said that he's less spooked when it comes to the supernatural and more wary of the living. "Places really don't freak me out," he mused, adding that he's had a few close encounters with wild animals when he taped *Ghost Hunters*. "Sometimes the clients themselves are frightening...the things that they say or do can be totally crazy."

Since retiring from *Ghost Hunters*, Berry continues to give paranormal-themed lectures with former on-air partner Amy Bruni. And recently, he's become a certified house hunter. Yes, he scored a real estate license and has launched a successful theatre company with his husband called Peregrine Theatre Ensemble.

For the record, the theatre's name is taken straight from Provincetown's Puritan-era history. "Peregrine White was the first child born to the Pilgrims in the New World while the *Mayflower* was anchored in Provincetown Harbor," Berry's website explained. "Our company's spirit embodies that same adventure and passion of braving uncharted possibilities."

LANCY MANSION

Provincetown's very own Norman Bates? Built by Benjamin R. Lancy Sr. for his mother in the late 1880s, the mansion was designed to emulate a Beacon Hill brownstone and towers over Commercial Street behind Cortile Gallery at 230 Commercial Street.

"Opposite the remnants of Lancy's Wharf behind Colonial Cold Storage is a magnificently eccentric Second Empire pile built in 1874 for Benjamin Lancy, a merchant and ship owner," reported the Provincetown Historical Commission, noting that the aesthetically creepy structure has an *Addams Family* vibe to it. "After Lancy Jr. died in 1923, the building was acquired by the Research Club, a history-minded civic group, to be used as the historical museum."

According to the Historical Commission online, the Lancy family was notorious for its eccentricity. "Local legend credits his father, also Benjamin Lancy, with refusing to allow Commercial Street to be laid out in a straight line in the West End," continued the report.

Lancy's approach to building the creepy mansion was just as odd as his public persona. The house was designed "using a process that he had discovered and invented to finish wood so that it resembled the then-fashionable brownstone," reported the *Advocate*. "With this method of treating wood, he hoped to make a fortune, and although he did manage to accumulate a sizeable amount of money, none of it came from his discovery."

Apparently, the house was "considered ugly," wrote the *Advocate*. However, "in time, people softened toward it."

The mother, known as "Grandma Lancy" or Nabby by the locals, wanted the tallest house in Provincetown, reported the newspaper, but "died before it was completed."

The woman specifically asked her son for a "widow's watch," or a cupola, so she could "keep account of the goings and comings of all ships in the harbor," as well as a bird's-eye view of the neighbors, reported historian and family descendent Louise Holbrook in the *Advocate*. "Lancy found an old ship's carpenter repairing ship's stairs in one of the Lancy's vessels. It was the only kind of stairs he ever built. So he built ship's stairs in the cupola of the Lancy mansion," she added.

The beloved Nabby passed on February 27, 1896. However, the macabre part of the story isn't the way the old matriarch died but what happened to her after her death.

Lancy kept his dead mother in the house for months "because a grave could not be dug in the frozen ground," Holbrook explained.

Built by Benjamin Lancy for his mother in the late 1880s, the Lancy Mansion was designed to emulate a Beacon Hill brownstone and is home to a lady-in-black ghost, who reportedly peeks out of the mansion's windows. *Photo by Sam Baltrusis.*

"When spring came the body was still in the upstairs front bedroom... until the neighbors complained. Family tradition relates that, due to public pressure, they finally buried their beloved mother three months after her death."

According to a letter from her great-great-granddaughter, the windows were kept open to chill the room and to keep the stench of death out of the house.

Six months after his mother's passing, Lancy's opera-singing wife had had enough and left the momma's boy. She returned to her wealthy family in Providence, Rhode Island. Mr. Lancy's son, reportedly even more eccentric than his father, inherited the house.

The strange habits of the Lancy men became Provincetown legend. "He was used to going swimming when he felt like it, sans bathing trunks," Holbrook wrote. "Even when he was an old man, he would come out of his Lancy mansion, walk straight down to the water, take off his clothes and swim nude. But no one paid any attention in 1912."

For the record, there was nothing between the mansion and the Provincetown Harbor "but a sandy front yard to Lancy's own wharf, for he owned a small fleet of ships—some for fishing and some for cargo."

Lancy Jr. became a recluse, known to collect horse dung for heating fuel. "He closed the house with its pretentious furnishings, and together with his sister, moved into the basement where they lived in miserly frugality," reported the *Cape-Cod Standard Times*. Lore suggested that the spirits inhabiting the twenty-room, brownstone-looking structure drove Lancy Jr. mad.

Passersby have spotted the apparition of a lady in black peeking out of the mansion's upstairs front bedroom and cupola. It's the spot where Lancy Sr. propped up his dead mother during the winter as they patiently waited for the cemetery's ground to thaw.

Jeannie Dougherty and Charles MacPherson, two former tenants who shared the top floor apartment at the Lancy Mansion in the 1990s, said they spent many sleepless nights in the creepy house. "They often witnessed lights turning on and off seemingly of their own volition. On one occasion, a hairdryer, which was put away in the closet, turned on by itself," reported *Cape Encounters*. "One afternoon when Charles was alone in the apartment he saw in the bathroom mirror somebody walking by behind him."

Dougherty, who roomed above the mansard roof near the staircase leading up to the widow's watch, said she heard phantom footsteps, implying a residual haunting, leading up to her room. "I literally froze in terror as I heard footsteps come straight up my stairs toward my bedroom door and then stop," she said. "I was too afraid to leave my

According to lore, Benjamin Lancy propped up his dead mother in the cupola of the Lancy Mansion during the winter as they patiently waited for the cemetery's ground to thaw. *Photo by Sam Baltrusis.*

room, but I can assure you I had every light on in the room that night and didn't sleep."

There's significance to the hairdryer mysteriously turning on in the closet.

Visitors, specifically women, who have visited the art gallery beneath the Lancy Mansion, claim to have felt the sensation of their hair being touched. Some even say they felt as if their locks were being brushed or groomed by an unseen force.

Adding to the tale from the crypt, after her death Lancy would brush his mother's hair, chatting with her as if she was still alive. Letters from family members confirmed the tale, claiming that Lancy combed the decaying woman's hair and even cut her nails.

Widow's Watch

PROVINCETOWN LIBRARY

Formerly the largest Methodist church in the country, the Provincetown Library's 1860-era building originally boasted a 162-foot steeple, but it was shortened to 100 feet after the Portland Gale. It was the tallest structure in Provincetown until the Pilgrim Monument was unveiled in 1910. The ghost of Captain Marion Perry, who won the Lipton Cup in August 1907, is rumored to haunt the half-scale replica of the *Rose Dorothea* schooner in the library. In the past, employees found clocks, which oddly resembled the ship's old-school compass, inexplicably lying on the floor when they opened the library in the morning.

Located at 356 Commercial Street, the library building's history is just as interesting as the structure's supposed ghostly inhabitants. Costing $22,000 to complete and boasting 128 pews, it was reputedly the largest Methodist denomination in the United States. More than 900 people could fit into the structure and the original tower, built in 1860, contained a larger-than-life bronze bell cast by George Holbrook.

For the record, the town's other Methodist church, called Centenary, located at 170 Commercial Street, had an equally tall spire, reaching 165 feet, but was tragically destroyed when a bolt of lightning struck the tower in the wee hours of March 14, 1908. "For two hours, the fire burned feebly and appeared to be confined in the steeple," wrote Irma Ruchstuhl in *Old Provincetown in Early Photographs*. "By 5 a.m. the great church was reduced to a heap of charred wood." According to the Provincetown Fire Department, the steeple fell at 3:00 a.m. nearly killing a dozen firemen. The structure was rebuilt and is now Joe Coffee & Cafe.

In 1958, the town's Methodist congregation sold the future Provincetown Library building to the son of the Chrysler Corporation, Walter P. Chrysler Jr. He transformed the building into an art museum and, after a twelve-year run, left because of a lack of parking in the East End part of town. The building stood vacant for four years. In 1974, it was turned into a "Center for the Arts," but it was short lived. In July 1976, it was acquired by the city and turned into a Heritage Museum. It was during this era that the *Rose Dorothea* replica was built.

In April 2005, the Provincetown Public Library moved in and set up shop. They kept a lot of the artifacts from the building's Heritage Museum days, including the reportedly enchanted *Rose Dorothea* and the 1907 Silver Lipton cup.

The trophy is supposedly the source of ghostly energy. Apparently the *Rose Dorothea's* captain, Marion Perry, was a notorious hothead

The creepy statue greeting passersby on Commercial Street is called *Tourists* and was sculpted by Chaim Gross. *Photo by Sam Baltrusis.*

Aerial view of the backside of the Provincetown Library, which is home to the half-scale replica of the *Rose Dorothea* schooner believed to be haunted by captain Marion Perry. *Courtesy Boston Public Library, Print Department.*

and it's possible he psychically imprinted his venomous energy on the silver race cup. "Captain Marion Perry, folks say, won the Lipton Cup because he was in a rage," reported *Time and the Town: A Provincetown Chronicle*. "When he was trying out the *Rose Dorothea* the topmast broke. Captain Marion Perry was not chary of words when he told the boat builder what he thought of his rotten spar." Apparently, during the race, his spar broke again and it's said that Perry "drove his vessel hotfoot to Boston," not in a brave attempt to win the Lipton Cup but to chew out the shipbuilder.

When he won the top prize, there was talk of keeping the silver trophy at the State House in Boston. Perry wouldn't have it. "What good would that damn cup do me in the State House?" he said. "I want it in my own Town Hall where my folks can get some good out of it."

During the victory parade honoring Perry and his crew, the *Boston Herald* reported that "during all the triumphal march, Captain Perry sat mute." He also dissed President Theodore Roosevelt when he was in Provincetown to lay the cornerstone of the Pilgrim Monument.

When asked about his absence, Captain Perry reportedly said: "If the President wants to see me he knows where to find me."

According to a story in the *Advocate*, a photo of Captain Perry from 1907 shows him "at the boat's wheel wearing a suit coat, a square-set derby hat, a handlebar mustache and a bulldog expression."

One explanation for Captain Perry's passive-aggressive actions is that evidence has surfaced suggesting that Perry was not, in fact, at the helm of the *Rose Dorothea* during the Lipton Cup race.

According to the *Duxbury Clipper* from July 5, 2006, a man named John Watson took over the ship's wheel after the topmast snapped off. Captain Watson was honored posthumously at a rededication ceremony at the Provincetown Library in 2006.

Oddly, it was around the time of the rededication that the poltergeist-like activities on the second floor of the library stopped. Reports of the ghostly shenanigans at the former Heritage Museum building—like the replica of the *Rose Dorothea*'s ship wheel mysteriously turning without provocation and clocks inexplicably falling off the wall—only stopped after it was announced that Captain Perry wasn't the winning captain.

"While it's a lovely building, I spent a lot of time at the Provincetown Library and asked workers there if they encountered any paranormal activity or ever bumped into a sea captain with a handlebar mustache and a derby hat," joked Jeffrey Doucette from Haunted Ptown. "No luck. Maybe the captain's spirit moved on or maybe it's just not an active building?"

Or perhaps the sea-captain specter that's been seen looking out toward the harbor from the spire of the Provincetown Library is, in fact, the ghost of Captain Watson seeking post-mortem recognition. Yes, it's feasible that once it was publicly announced that Captain Watson won the Lipton Cup, not Captain Perry, Watson was finally able to rest in peace.

FILE UNDER

Rose *Ruse*

UNITARIAN UNIVERSALIST MEETINGHOUSE

Used as an infirmary during the flu epidemic of 1918, the Unitarian Universalist Meetinghouse (UUMH) was built in 1847 and is reportedly one of Provincetown's more paranormally active locations. "People say that they've seen a woman in full colonial garb walking across the sanctuary," explained Adam Berry, formerly of *Ghost Hunters*. "They also hear singing when no one is there. When I was doing a fundraiser in the building one night, I heard distinct footsteps walk across the church's pulpit."

Other sources, like *Uncommon Sense Media*, have echoed Berry's observation that UUMH is indeed active. "It meets all the criteria for being a haunted house because it's an old building and it has a creepy history. Like all haunted houses, people report seeing 'something' moving from the corner of their eye and also 'felt a presence' when alone."

Formerly called the Universalist Church of the Redeemer, the striking white structure located at 236 Commercial Street was the crown jewel of Provincetown's spiritual community. "Every detail of the beautiful Christopher Wren tower and the facade with its dignified simplicity with the great spruces on either side, make an unforgettable picture," reported *New Beacon* in 1962. "Inside the church is the same beautiful sanctuary, just as it was in 1847, when it was built, with the same priceless Sandwich glass chandeliers."

The structure's acoustics are to die for and oddly accentuate the church's more notorious spirits: singing specters.

The Unitarian Universalist Meetinghouse is "notable for having a ghostly choir," confirmed *Cape Encounters*. According to the account, the building's historian was alone downstairs in the meetinghouse when she claimed to have heard the ghost group singing. "She waited ten minutes before daring to walk upstairs to confirm the source. When she reached the top of the stairs, she found the second floor quiet and empty."

The church's former sexton, Oscar, had a face-to-face to encounter with the ghostly choir. "His memory included recollections of looking up and seeing the ensemble dressed in coats," *Cape Encounters* continued.

So, why a ghost choir?

One theory is that the ghosts of the Commercial Street haunt are somehow tied to the Great Pandemic of 1918. The plague started in Boston on August 27 when several sailors were stricken with a deadly flu virus. In three days, there were fifty-eight cases in Boston and it quickly spread to 2,000 people within two weeks.

"This epidemic started about four weeks ago, and has developed so rapidly that the camp is demoralized and all ordinary work is held up till

Used as a morgue during the great plague, the Unitarian Universalist Meetinghouse was built in 1847. Hauntings include a spectral choir. *Photo by Sam Baltrusis.*

it has passed," reported a beleaguered physician from nearby Camp Devens. "These men start with what appears to be an ordinary attack of influenza and when brought to the hospital they very rapidly develop the most viscous type of pneumonia that has ever been seen. Two hours after admission they have the mahogany spots over the cheekbones, and a few hours later you can begin to see the cyanosis extending from their ears and spreading all over the face. It is only a matter of a few hours then until death comes, and it is simply a struggle for air until they suffocate. It is horrible."

The killer flu quickly traveled to Provincetown and locals felt under siege. "In 1918, came the flu epidemic. Then Provincetown put on a strange face," wrote Mary Heaton Vorse in *A Time and the Town: A Provincetown Chronicle*. "Everyone went around masked with an antiseptic cloth. It made one feel that the days of pestilence in the Middle Ages had returned. People were stricken so fast that hospitals couldn't care for them. A hospital was improvised in the Universalist Church."

More than 45,000 people in Massachusetts over a four-month period. According to Vorse, at least twenty-five died at the Universalist church.

Eyewitnesses who have encountered the ghost choir said they've seen around two dozen apparitions in this ghostly chorus. Based on reports, it's possible that these spirited songbirds are a residual haunting from the Pandemic flu era. Oddly, the numbers of those who died at the church correlate to the spirits participating in the ghost-choir ensemble.

And what about the female apparition wearing Colonial garb? One idea is that she's just passing through, which is common for an energy not bound to a specific location. Another possibility is that she's linked to the *Mayflower*. Dorothy Bradford drowned on December 7, 1620, in Provincetown Harbor. Legend suggests it was a depression-induced suicide. However, it's more likely that she accidentally fell off the vessel into the freezing harbor while her husband, William Bradford, was searching for suitable land to build a colony. The spot where the meetinghouse currently resides was marshland in the 1600s and it's possible that the Colonial-era woman washed ashore in the present-day vicinity of the church.

Singing Specters

CHAPTER 2

CRIME HAUNTS

I t's the cold case that has haunted Provincetown for forty years. The Lady of the Dunes' severely mutilated corpse was found on a secluded service road near Dunes' Edge Campground at Race Point Beach on July 26, 1974. On the day the body was discovered, the buzzing insects sounded like muted screams, alluding to the horrors that unfolded in the wooded area almost a half of a century ago.

Human monsters once roamed here.

The ghost of Provincetown's most infamous gone girl has haunted Sandra Lee, author of *The Shanty* and a Provincetown regular since the 1970s. The crime writer was only nine-years-old when she claimed to have stumbled on the cold case of the century. According to Lee, the Lady of the Dunes' decomposing body continues to haunt her dreams. During an emotional discussion that stirred up childhood demons, Lee told *Paranormal Provincetown* that the woman's dead body sounded like a string of pearls rubbing together.

"She was in the brush, in the seagrass about fifteen feet from an access road," Lee recalled. "The road follows the backside of Dunes' Edge Campground. She was in the thick of the brush. It was nothing shy of horrific. It was something I will never forget."

Lee, who camped at Dunes' Edge every July in the early '70s, said it has taken her years to talk publicly about the horrors from her childhood. While there is a local teenage girl on record who is credited with calling responding officers to the scene in 1974, the fifty-year-old author said she and her sister found the rotting corpse of the Lady of the Dunes two days before police were alerted.

"I stumbled down an incline with my dog," she continued. "The dog was ahead of me. My dog got excited about something. I heard a very

Author Sandra Lee wrote a fictionalized account in 2011 about the Lady of the Dunes case, called "The Shanty." Lee is standing next to the victim's grave in Provincetown's St. Peter's Cemetery. *Courtesy Sandra Lee.*

strange noise. If you could imagine someone holding a string of pearls, I heard that sound. And then there was a horrible smell. At first, I attributed it to low tide," said Lee with emotion as she recollected the horrific scene. "She was face down. Her hair was a mess and I could see a gouge in the right side of her neck. Her arms were tucked down in the sand so I didn't know anything was missing. I recognized the green blanket right away. The lower half of her body was covered with something."

Lee said the horrible sound has stayed with her for years. "It wasn't until much later that I realized that the sound of someone playing with a pearl necklace was from the maggots," she said. "Her body was covered with maggots. I believe there were a few people who found the body, but there is only one who spoke to police in person about it."

On July 26, 1974, a girl who was walking her dog discovered the naked, decomposing body of a woman in her twenties or early thirties. The body was lying face down wearing Wrangler jeans with a blue bandana placed crudely under her head. A green blanket was also found at the scene. The murder victim had long auburn or reddish-colored hair clamped in a glittery, elastic-band ponytail and was approximately five-foot-six inches tall. She had an athletic build and was approximately 135 pounds. The Lady of the Dunes, as she has been nicknamed, had extensive dental work done on her teeth, worth thousands of dollars. The killer had removed several of the teeth—a practice that James "Whitey" Bulger and his cronies were known for. Her hands had been removed and she had been nearly decapitated with what is believed to have been a military entrenching tool. She had also received massive trauma to the side of her skull. Police believed she had been sexually assaulted.

Oddly, the gruesome crime scene became the single most visited tourist attraction in Provincetown during its peak season in the summer of 1974.

Provincetown became a safe haven for lesbians and gay men in the late 1960s and early '70s. There were several LGBT friendly bars, including the A-House, which "turned gay" in 1976, the Pilgrim House, Ptown's earliest drag bar called Weathering Heights, The Moors, and of course, the Crown & Anchor.

Lee reminisced about the early '70s with fondness. "Before 1974, I remember drinking out of glass Coke bottles and eating candy apples," she said, adding that there was a dark side to the town's picturesque facade. "It wasn't fun for me after 1974. In the '70s, Provincetown was a huge port for money, drugs, and human trafficking. Whitey has a history of bisexuality. Gay-related crimes were often overlooked in the '70s. At the time, people weren't on to Whitey's trips to Provincetown. It was his playground and no one knew he was doing half of the things he was doing here. It was the perfect place for the disposal of the body."

Lee said her stepfather, a violent alcoholic, would spend nights at the Crown & Anchor with Bulger while her family camped at Dunes' Edge. "Not many people knew that Bulger was hanging out in Provincetown, nor did they realize he was a switch hitter," Lee said. "My stepfather would stumble into the campsite during the wee morning hours. He was always inebriated and disheveled, often bruised and bloody, and sometimes wearing a green cotton blanket around his shoulders, which he'd taken from the inn."

The author said that she fears her stepfather may have been at the scene, as he often interacted with Bulger in Milton and Provincetown. "Whether it was my stepfather, I don't know. It was too coincidental that we camped there. If you rolled off the embankment, there she was," Lee said. "The reason why I found her was because I was running from a bad situation. Finding her certainly put things in perspective for me because obviously she was in a much worse situation. In a sense, she helped save my life. Coming from an abusive home environment, I thought this was as bad as it gets. But, when you stumbled on what I did you realize that what happened to the Lady of the Dunes is as bad as it gets."

The Provincetown Police Department (PPD) claimed in previous interviews that several witnesses and photographs have placed Bulger in the area at the time of the murder. However, Lee responded saying "nothing concrete has yet tied Bulger to the Provincetown murder, but he has not yet been ruled out as a suspect." The PPD followed up on several initial leads that pointed to local individuals as well as two serial killers, including Tony "Chop Chop" Costa. However, the notorious murderer committed suicide in 1970. The theories were all proven wrong.

Bulger, eighty-four, was captured in Santa Monica, California, after more than sixteen years on the run. Fleeing Boston in 1995, he was charged with participating in nineteen murders as well as a slew of other horrific crimes. Stephen "The Rifleman" Flemmi, testified in federal court that Bulger lured twenty-six-year-old Deborah Hussey to a South Boston home in 1985. Flemmi claimed that Bulger strangled her. Following the trial, Bulger was sentenced to two consecutive terms of life in prison.

Did Bulger and his cronies kill the Lady of the Dunes? Lee believed she was one of the South Boston gang's victims. However, her main motivation is to find closure for the unidentified woman.

Lee wrote a fictionalized account in 2011 about the Lady of the Dunes case, called *The Shanty*, while camping at Dunes' Edge Campground. "It was terribly difficult for me to write. I wrote about the case in fictional form because technically it was still a pending investigation. It was difficult for me to write because I had to revisit a lot of demons I thought

More than forty years after her murder, a metal casket in Provincetown's St. Peter's Cemetery contains the remains of the Lady of the Dunes. The gravestone is labeled "unidentified female." *Courtesy Sandra Lee.*

I left behind," she said. "In the long run, it was extremely cathartic for me. It was tough, but I tried to stay focused. I needed to go through so much healing before even writing this book."

Lee said the woman would appear in her dreams while she camped at Dunes' Edge Campground, implying that the woman's restless spirit still lingers in the area.

More than forty years after her murder, a metal casket in Provincetown's St. Peter's Cemetery contains the remains of the Lady of the Dunes. The gravestone is labeled as "unidentified female" and it's falling apart.

The author hopes detectives at the PPD can at least identify the murdered woman. "Let's remember her," Lee emoted. "We're running out of time. Let's try to give this woman a name. Everybody deserves a name on their headstone. Keeping her in the forefront of the public eye will help solve this case. The only way to do it is to keep the story alive."

TOWN HALL

Adam Berry, formerly of *Ghost Hunters*, swears that Provincetown's town hall is chock-full of ghosts. "It used to be an old jail and the people who work there say that the offices downstairs are haunted," Berry said, adding that the town hall's former jail once housed Marlon Brando, who spent the night in the drunk tank after playing bongos on the street. "I don't have proof but people say that it's active. During construction employees claimed that tools and ladders were moved [by an unseen force] and that you could hear disembodied voices, which makes sense because construction usually brings up activity."

The original town hall was on High Pole Hill at the present site of the Pilgrim Monument. It was destroyed by fire on February 16, 1877. The current structure was built in 1880 and cost around $50,000.

"For years, town hall's basement served as Provincetown's jail. Not intended for long-term prisoners, the cells in the basement were quintessential 'pokey' where many revelers, who were too drunk to find their way home, spent the night to 'sleep it off,'" confirmed *Provincetown Magazine*. "Those cells, which held the likes of Marlon Brando and Eugene O'Neill, were preserved during the renovations. The bars and bricks are nicely incorporated into the town's building department office."

According to the team from Manchester Paranormal Investigations in New Hampshire, the first question they ask when people contact them about an alleged haunting is whether the location has recently been renovated. "A spirit may or may not like the changes being made to his or her environment. One thing to remember is a spirit who has remained behind has some anchors that makes them bound or choose to remain in this realm," explained the investigative team. "Sometimes the spirit likes to remain in a comfortable environment since oftentimes a spirit may be confused, angry, or in a poor state of mind. When their familiar surrounding becomes a bit chaotic, as is often the case with renovations, they become a bit uncomfortable. For those that do not realize they are dead, suddenly their surroundings are changing without explanation."

Spirits unhappy with the changes to a historic location will meddle with construction, like moving ladders or causing objects like paint brushes or power tools to disappear.

Joni Mayhan, a paranormal researcher and author of *Bones in the Basement* and *Devil's Toy Box*, told *Paranormal Provincetown* that the two-year, $6 million renovation project to town hall from 2008 to 2010 could have conjured up activity. "Yes, it's not unusual for a construction project to stir up paranormal activity that might have previously been dormant," Mayhan explained. "I see this frequently in older houses and

During renovations of Old Town Hall, employees claimed that tools and ladders were moved by an unseen force. *Photo by Sam Baltrusis.*

buildings. If a person loved a location so much they didn't want to leave it, even after death, they often take offense when those living there decide to make changes."

Mayhan said she has first-hand experience with spirits making a post-mortem protest against a renovation project. "We gutted the basement of our first house, removing an old work bench that had obviously been used for decades by someone who had lived in the house before us," she continued. "Not long afterwards, we began hearing footsteps in empty rooms and began seeing shadows move that had no explanation. I've seen it happen over and over again with others, as well. Sometimes the dead don't mind sharing our space, but they aren't always happy when we decide to alter it from the way it once was."

Jeffrey Doucette, founder of the Haunted Ptown ghost tour, said town workers are still creeped out about the structure's basement. "While inquiring about permitting, I was directed to speak with one of the departments down in the basement," Doucette recalled. "For a period of time, the basement held the town jail. It's rumored to be haunted. During my conversation with someone within the permits office, a woman who worked in the building interrupted my conversation and said, 'I don't know what's down here, but I don't like being down here alone. It creeps me out.'" When Doucette asked her why the space scared her, she sheepishly explained: "I always feel like there is someone down here with me."

So, who or what is haunting the basement of Town Hall? No one knows for sure. However, paranormal experts suggest that it's likely someone who died unexpectedly when the jail served as a drunk tank. Someone like Zeke Cabal, who was known for his drunken shenanigans in the 1920s, could have left a psychic imprint of sorts on the location.

Or, if big names pique your interest, it could be *On the Waterfront* icon and legendary bad boy, Marlon Brando, playing his bongos in the afterlife. He spent one helluva night in the makeshift jail. Yes, he could be a contender.

Haunted Hall

VICTORIA HOUSE

Guests at Provincetown's Victoria House, located at 5 Standish Street, reported "uneasy feelings in the middle of the night accompanied with the smell of blood," Provincetown Paranormal Research Society posted. "Apparently it was once the home to a doctor or butcher?"

Oddly, Victoria House was, in fact, the residence of the town's butcher. His name was Tony "Chop Chop" Costa.

Provincetown's first street car, the "Pilgrim," trekked down Standish Street to its final destination at the wooden MacMillan Pier, which was built in 1873. The Victoria House bed and breakfast's name is a bit misleading. "I thought the house was Victorian, thus the name. But it was a misnomer as the house is definitely not Victorian," said the former owner who purchased it in 1972.

Every major town or city has one: a murder house. In Provincetown, it's known as the Victoria House.

Once owned by Provincetown's sheriff, it was turned into a guest house in the 1960s and the infamous serial killer Tony Costa stayed

Tony Costa's crimes were particularly gruesome. Costa was staying in Room 4 of the Victoria House when he met and then murdered two women. *Photo by Sam Baltrusis.*

Formerly owned by Provincetown's sheriff and turned into a flophouse in the 1960s, the Victoria House, located at 5 Standish Street, also once housed serial killer "Tony Chop Chop" Costa. *Photo by Sam Baltrusis.*

in what is now Room 4. Antone Charles Costa, known by the locals as Tony "Chop Chop" Costa, was convicted in 1970 of the murder of two young women—that of Patricia H. Walsh and Mary Ann Wysocki—although he is believed to have killed two more. The house for a brief period was often pointed out to tourists as the site where the murderer lived. Also, sand from the gruesome grave site was sold to gawkers for half a buck.

The Provincetown-based carpenter met his two confirmed victims at the building then called the Guest House.

Costa's crimes were particularly gruesome. The heart of each girl was removed and was not found at the grave site. Each corpse was cut into parts. While the discovery of the victims caused a sensation, it was apparently the District Attorney Edmund Dinis' description of the remains that caused the initial uproar. "A razor like device was found near the graves," Dinis announced. "Each body was cut into as many parts as there are joints." There were also teeth marks found on the bodies.

Kurt Vonnegut Jr. discussed the case in *Life* magazine on July 25, 1969, and the story became a national sensation. "Jack the Ripper used to get compliments about the way he dissected the women he killed," wrote Vonnegut. "Now Cape Cod has a mutilator. The pieces of four young women were found in a shallow grave. Whoever did it was no artist with the knife. He chopped up the women with what the police guess was a brush hook or an ax. It couldn't have taken too long to do."

Vonnegut talked about "stained rope" that was found at the scene. The evidence was similar to the bloody coil found in Costa's closet in his room at 5 Standish Street. The *Slaughterhouse-Five* author also captured the vibe of Provincetown in this well-crafted story, mentioning telling observations including graffiti painted on a Truro laundromat: "Tony Costa digs girls."

He also poked fun at the thrillseekers. "When the bodies were found last winter, tourists arrived off-season," he wrote. "They wanted to help dig. They were puzzled when park rangers and police and firemen found them disgusting."

The story almost became the crime of the century. However, Charlie Manson's "Helter Skelter" murder spree in California trumped Costa's chopping frenzy. The "secret garden" killer was sentenced to life in prison and ended up committing suicide by hanging himself in his cell on May 12, 1974.

As for hauntings, there have been reports of residual energy in Room 4. According to a former manager at the Victoria House, he would hear disembodied whispers throughout the guest house and the occasional scream of a female voice emanating from Room 4. Some believe that Costa may have kept his victims in the Victoria House, similar to Buffalo Bill in *Silence of the Lambs*, before murdering them, removing their hearts and burying them in Truro.

"In the guest house on Standish Street, near the center of town, the slain girls checked in for a night last January," the *Life* piece explained. "At the time, Tony Costa was renting a room there by the week. He was introduced to the other guests by the landlady, Mrs. Patricia Morton."

The girls checked in, but they never checked out.

Jeffrey Doucette from Haunted Ptown said the stories involving Provincetown's "very own serial killer" were an unexpected point of interest. "On one tour, I had just told my group that no one would jump out and frighten them," he recalled. "Boy, was I wrong. As I was about to talk about the Victoria House, I stepped into the street and there, lying between two parked cars, was a young man...wearing a black cloak. I let out a yelp as this was a total surprise to me. The young man realized he had startled me and some others on the tour, apologized to the group and walked away. Everyone on the tour said, 'Okay, that was weird.'"

Doucette said several locals came up to him, including legendary *Serial Mom* director and author John Waters, to share stories involving Tony "Chop Chop" Costa. "The famous filmmaker informed me that Mink Stole had gone on a date with Tony Costa," Doucette mused. "Luckily, she made it back without any problems."

Chop Shop

WHYDAH PIRATE MUSEUM

The Whydah Pirate Museum at 16 Macmillan Wharf, boasts some priceless treasures believed to be cursed by a love-lost pirate keeping an eye on his stolen 300-year-old booty.

The recovered gold from the pirate ship *Whydah* (pronounced "widdah"), which sank in a violent storm off Cape Cod in 1717, is rumored to be enchanted by "Black Sam" Bellamy. Apparently, the notorious pirate captain is still protecting his loot, which includes over 10,000 coins and 400 pieces of Akan gold jewelry.

According to paranormal researchers who believe in the Stone Tape theory, inanimate objects such as a pirate's treasure can absorb a form of energy from living people during intense moments in those people's lives.

"A residual haunting—trapped energy—is more likely stored by an item near the event," explained the authors of *Haunted Objects: Stories of Ghosts on Your Shelf.* "It becomes almost like a character...a crystal lamp or a setting of silverware becomes haunted and then replays the moment when the right tumblers fall into place. The object can be moved to another location and when the situation is right, the recording replays, creating a haunting."

The story behind Bellamy's enchanted treasure is rife with eighteenth-century drama.

"Sam Bellamy was in love. The object of his affection, according to Cape Cod lore, was Maria Hallett of Eastham, Massachusetts. Her parents liked Sam well enough but didn't think a poor sailor would make much of a husband. So, in 1715, Bellamy went looking for his fortune," reported *National Geographic.* "He and his friend Palgrave Williams started out as ordinary treasure hunters, looking for shipwrecks. They found none. Rather than return empty-handed, the legend said, the determined lover became a pirate—"Black Sam" Bellamy. It was the perfect job for him. In just a year of raiding, Bellamy and his crew plundered more than fifty ships on the Caribbean and Atlantic. They were getting rich—quick."

Based on the legend, the twenty-eight-year-old pirate with jet-black hair captured the three-masted ship *Whydah.* The vessel boasted 20,000 pounds sterling of silver and gold earned from the lucrative sale of slaves, according to *National Geographic.* But the blood money was cursed: Bellamy's ship sank near the coast of Wellfleet on April 16, 1717. It's claimed that the pirate was holding onto his beloved gold as the stolen ship sank in a violent storm within a short distance of the Cape Cod shoreline.

Argh matey! The Whydah Pirate Museum, located at 16 Macmillan Wharf, contains recovered pirate treasure rumored to be enchanted by "Black Sam" Bellamy. *Photo by Sam Baltrusis.*

While Bellamy was smitten with his booty, his love for Hallett was epic. Stories about his heartbroken girlfriend range from the absurd—like the fact that she was so resentful about his death that she sold her soul to the devil and became a witch—to the tragic. One story, told by Peter Muise in *New England Folklore*, suggested that "Maria remained faithful to Sam, watching and waiting patiently for his return. On the night of the storm she watched from the dunes, hoping the *Whydah* would make it safely to shore. When it didn't, she lost her mind from grief and ran down to the beach. The next day she was found on the shore, screaming and wailing as she wandered through the wreckage and drowned corpses."

Muise claimed that "her ghost is still said to walk near Marconi Beach in Wellfleet and her cries can be heard on dark stormy nights."

One twist on the story suggested that Hallett and Bellamy consummated their fiery romance and she gave birth to his child. "Maria was said to have given birth to a boy with black hair," wrote Mark Jasper in *Haunted Cape Cod*. "When she became pregnant she moved to a secluded spot in order to conceal her pregnancy, as townspeople of that era had no tolerance for unwed mothers." The child died in a freak accident by choking on straw, and Hallett was sent to prison for neglect. She escaped and was then called a witch.

Jasper also suggested that Hallett's ghost walks the dunes of Wellfleet. "Eyewitnesses have seen the ghostly apparition of a woman walking the cliffs and peering out at the sea for a lover who would never return," he wrote.

Apparently, Hallett's wailing specter has been spotted in various other locations throughout the Outer Cape. In 1998, a patron at a restaurant in Wellfleet claimed that the apparition of a young, blonde female had approached her in the restroom. Oddly, the woman who experienced this face-to-face encounter with Hallett's supposed ghost had a familiar last name: Bellamy.

And "Black Sam" has not been able to rest in peace, either. "Spirits associated with the *Whydah* continue to linger nearly three centuries later," wrote the Houston Museum of Natural Science. "Barry Clifford, discoverer of the *Whydah's* remains, recounts in his book, *Expedition Whydah*, how the start of his 1998 exploration was plagued with constant, often inexplicable obstacles—engine problems, an undermanned crew, GPS malfunction, heavy fog, a shark encounter, and more."

One crew member on Clifford's salvage vessel claimed that an eerie voice from beyond was heard over the radio speaker near the wreck site. The voice kept repeating: "We want your boat.... We want your boat." Clifford's crew was so creeped out they poured a bottle of rum overboard to make peace with the pirates. Apparently, it worked because the treasure hunters recovered the gold.

But the hauntings haven't stopped. The salty sentinel spirit at *Whydah* Pirate Museum in Provincetown is said to watch over the treasure. Bellamy called. He wants his booty back.

Paranormal Pirate

Harbor view from the allegedly haunted Whydah Pirate Museum. *Photo by Sam Baltrusis.*

CHAPTER 3

NIGHTLIFE HAUNTS

Michael Baker, head of the scientific group called the New England Center for the Advancement of Paranormal Science (NECAPS), leaves no gravestone unturned when he investigates a so-called haunted location, which includes the Martin House in Provincetown, a former nightlife haunt turned private residence.

In fact, Baker's "real science, real answers" mantra cuts through the usual smoke and mirrors associated with the "Boo!" business. With Baker, there's no over-the-top *Ghostbusters* gear or fake Cockney accents. When it comes to science-based paranormal investigations, Baker is the real deal.

"Basically, there is no ghost-catching device," explained Baker. "The field has changed. It has taken more of a fun-house approach—it has become a novelty—and it has set the paranormal investigation field back in a way. A lot of people are trying to use a screwdriver to hammer a nail. People go in with preconceived notions, and if anything happens, they're going to come to a certain conclusion. If something moves, bumps or they hear footsteps, they're going to automatically assume that it's a ghost, and that's a bad way to investigate."

Baker continued: "Technology can't detect spirits...we have to prove that spirits exist before we can build anything that can measure them. There was a shift in the field, occurring in the '90s, where it's a game to mimic what is seen on television. There was a period where it was purely scientific, and now people think they can turn off the lights, pick up an infrared camera and capture a ghost."

Soon after the Martin House Restaurant was sold and turned into a private residence, he led an investigation with a small crew.

Paranormal scientist Michael Baker, who investigated the Martin House Restaurant in Provincetown, shows off his homemade Electromagnetic Spectrum Sensor. *Photo by Sam Baltrusis.*

"Sadly our investigation was ruined by the owners inviting friends to the investigation and throwing a party," Baker said. "It was so noisy we had to discount all of our audio. There were two investigators at the time who claimed to have seen shadows in the attic. Unfortunately, they were not captured on tape."

Is it something in the water? The Native Americans called Provincetown "Meeshawn," which meant "where there is going by boat." A lot of the town's paranormal activity is related to its maritime history. "Claims of hauntings and the sea are legendary and water may have played some role in legitimate activity," Baker concluded.

Most of the alleged activity at haunted nightlife locales seems to be related to Provincetown's seafaring past. For example, *Cape Encounters* reported a residual haunting of a salty sea captain specter spotted beneath the Gifford House Inn at 11 Carver Street "Several housemen, receptionists and bartenders have seen a male figure sitting at a table in a basement dance club called Purgatory," *Cape Encounters* explained. "The specter, who wears a captain's hat, peacoat, and a red scarf, is said to strike a contemplative pose, looking downward while holding a pipe in his right hand up to his mouth, and leaning his left elbow on the table."

For the record, a former employee at the Gifford House, which is upstairs from Purgatory, said that several guests at the inn's piano bar lobby have reported a young ghost girl peeking out from behind chairs and furniture. She likes music, the source claimed, and her spirit is attracted to the bar's old-school piano.

Baker believes the geodynamics of Provincetown's soil may be a factor in its onslaught of supposed activity. "The arm of Massachusetts from Ptown to Bourne primarily consists of a foundation made up of unconsolidated sediment...meaning it's made up of a mash of organic materials containing calcite from seashells, minerals, pebbles of various stones, quartz and salts," he explained. "These elements are basically the same things found in limestone and sandstone, two stones believed to have paranormal properties," he said, adding that some believe "limestone induces paranormal activity."

It's this drive to scientifically quantify every piece of evidence that separates Baker's group from the rest of the paranormal-investigator pack. In fact, it's been his lifelong passion to find the truth after having a close encounter with the supernatural at his childhood home in Arlington. According to the researcher, his mother saw an apparition and he heard voices coming from his backyard. Several incidents when he was eight, involving inexplicable footsteps and slamming doors, have haunted him for years.

"There were all of these strange experiences where the bathroom door would slam shut and lock itself; it was a dead-bolt lock, and there's no way it could twist on its own," Baker explained. "Every week or so, we would hear footsteps, and we could actually see the impressions of a foot on the hardwood floors. One night, my sister and I heard a loud bang coming from the kitchen, and it sounded like the silverware drawer was being opened and slammed repeatedly. We walked in cautiously, peeked in and it stopped. We opened the drawer, and all of the silverware was shoved at the end of the drawer as if it was slammed shut repeatedly."

Baker, who is the resident skeptic in the series of historical-based ghost books that precede *Paranormal Provincetown*, said he still hasn't found what he's looking for when it comes to a science-based explanation. "I never got answers from my family as to why these things were happening, and we never talked about it until after we moved," he recalled. "I started reading books and never got the answers I was looking for. It wasn't just a childhood hallucination. There was something to it. I don't know what it is, and I still don't know what it is. I do know there is something and I'm going to find it."

ATLANTIC HOUSE

Built in 1798 by Provincetown's first postmaster, Daniel Pease, the Atlantic House (A-House) was the last stage-coach stop until 1873 for commuters coming in from Orleans. Formerly known as the Union House in the 1800s, it was also a regular watering hole for America's more infamous turn-of-the-century writers, including Eugene O'Neill and Tennessee Williams. According to several accounts, the now off-limits quarters upstairs at the A-House is a hotspot for paranormal activity.

"The A-House is definitely haunted," confirmed Ashley Shakespeare, a veteran ghost tour guide and regular performer in Provincetown. "There are residual haunts especially in the guest house. When I was in the cast of the show *Painted Ladies*, our dressing room was upstairs in the old guest house. Lights would turn on and doors would open and close."

Shakespeare, who is sensitive to the paranormal, said the activity at the Atlantic House isn't intelligent. The energy, he explained, is residual—or like a videotaped replay of past events. "I feel the A-House is most haunted with residual energy, from back when Judy Garland, Billie Holiday, Eartha Kitt, and so many other greats were entertaining there," he claimed. "I have been in the A-House during the day by myself and could feel this great energy and presence."

The excitement of past performers, he said, has left a psychic imprint on the historic structure. "It was almost as if a live band was coming up through the floor and an audience just started to appear buzzing about whichever great performer was about to appear," the drag illusionist continued. "It was magical."

Of course, the building's well-known former tenant, playwright Eugene O'Neill, could have left an indelible mark on the allegedly haunted guest house.

"In the late spring of 1917, O'Neill and his friend Harold DePolo, a pulp fiction writer and proficient drinking partner, were arrested on charges of espionage at the still-operating Atlantic House bar in Provincetown," explained Robert M. Dowling in his book, *Critical Companion to Eugene O'Neill*. "Secret Service agents were summoned from Boston, as the United States had just entered the First World War and there was a general scare of German spies on American soil. The bohemian vagabonds looked highly suspicious to local Provincetowners—particularly O'Neill, who was carrying a black satchel that appeared as if it might contain surveillance equipment but was most likely his typewriter case."

O'Neill spent the night in the basement of Provincetown's town hall, which is also reportedly haunted, but was released when O'Neill was identified as the son of his famous father, actor James O'Neill.

Built in 1798 by Provincetown's first postmaster Daniel Pease, the Atlantic House was the last stagecoach stop until 1873. The off-limits quarters upstairs is said to be a hotspot for paranormal activity. *Photo by Sam Baltrusis.*

Mary Heaton Vorse, author of *Time and the Town: A Provincetown Chronicle,* said that O'Neill was the subject of a full-blown witch hunt. "The poor man was persecuted," Vorse wrote. "There was talk of running him out town, of arresting him, when Max Bohm, the famous painter, came furiously to his assistance and shamed the witch-hunters into silence and sanity."

If O'Neill is, in fact, haunting the Atlantic House, he's double dipping in the afterlife.

Students at Kilachand Hall in Boston, formerly Shelton Hall, claim the playwright haunts the dorm's Writers' Corridor on the fourth floor. The *Long Day's Journey into Night* author—crippled with a slew of ailments ranging from a rare genetic neurological disease to tuberculosis to depression to stomach disorders exacerbated by alcoholism—spent the last two years of his life in suite 401 when the BU dormitory, located at 91 Bay State Road, was a Sheraton-owned hotel. Kilachand was originally built in 1923. Ironically, O'Neill was born in a hotel, the Barrett, located at 1500 Broadway in the heart of New York City's Times Square.

O'Neill spent his last days downing shots of whiskey in suite 401 to numb both his emotional and physical pain. He forced the liquor down his throat and, in essence, drank himself to death. His famous last words? "Born in a hotel room and goddammit, died in a hotel room," he reportedly whispered to his wife Carlotta three days before his final curtain call on November 27, 1953.

Carlotta, who moved into the building in 1951 because of its proximity to her shrink's office on Bay State Road, insisted that her husband's ghost was in the room and that he talked to her into the wee hours of the night.

Boston University purchased the Bay State Road structure in 1954, and Carlotta soon checked out. However, her famous husband's tortured soul is rumored to remain in Kilachand Hall. Reports of an elevator mysteriously stopping on the fourth floor, phantom knocks, unexplained gusts of wind, and inexplicably dim lights continue to creep out students who live there.

Oddly, the hauntings reported at the A-House's upstairs guest house echo the types of phenomenon at the Boston University dorm, including phantom knocking, inexplicable cold spots and doors opening and closing.

Is O'Neill taking a post-mortem vacation at his former haunt in Provincetown? Apparently, the show must go on—even in the afterlife.

Phantom Playwright

LOCAL 186

The Commercial Street restaurant had a past life as Esther's Inn, run by a Provincetown matriarch called Esther Chamberlain. The hotspot aimed "to capture all the glamour and ritzy sophistication that embodies her reputation," the magazine *Fodor's* reported. In the late 1980s, it was called the Painted Lady Inn. Esther reportedly haunts the building. In fact, there was a photo of the matriarch in the building when the restaurant was called Enzo's.

From a paranormal perspective, it's common for people who have built empires to stick around after their death.

Based on lore, the hard-working former owner seemed to be concerned with the success of 186 Commercial Street. "My theory is that when one person works so hard to build an empire, whether it's a city, a business or [Esther's Inn], they can still be around trying to check on what's going on and how those still there are running the place," said Provincetown's Adam Berry, claiming that he's heard numerous reports of Esther still running the show at her former business. "I believe Provincetown has tons of spirits. People were building empires, and the more energy that surrounds that kind of situation the more likely there will be spirits lingering about."

A post on *Building Provincetown* confirmed the rumors, adding that the five-room guest house that overlooks the restaurant and Grotta Bar formerly owned by Esther and her husband Stanley Chamberlain is still called Enzo's. However, the dining room is now called Local 186. "Named for the great Italian automobile racer and manufacturer, Enzo Ferrari, this establishment is a restaurant, a guest house (five rooms) and a bar (Grotta). This was formerly Esther's Inn, run by Esther Chamberlain," the website explained. "The building is reportedly haunted."

Michael Baker, a scientific paranormal investigator with the group Para-Boston, said there isn't any rhyme or reason why a location like Local 186 would be active versus another Provincetown-based haunt. "When we are speaking of interactions with activity alleged to be connected to the existing consciousness of human beings, I would think a more active history would always play a bigger role," Baker explained. "However, in my findings I have not yet seen a correlation between the type of historic activity and proposed hauntings. Much of the connections of violent pasts to haunted locations seems to be more folklore than fact. I'm still not sure what elements of our daily lives leave the biggest impacts."

In other words, Baker believes that a place like Esther's Inn has as much potential to be paranormally active as other locations with a richer history or a violent past. "The claims of hauntings by the majority seems

Located at 186 Commercial Street, Local 186 had a past life as Esther's Inn, run by Provincetown matriarch Esther Chamberlain. *Photo by Sam Baltrusis.*

to be void of elements that directly tie to major historical events," he said, using his data-focused NECAPS report as proof. "We never see Lincoln giving the Gettysburg address for example, and while the battlefields in Gettysburg do seem to produce alleged remnants of battles, that trait does not seem to continue in many other violent locations where paranormal activity is simply footsteps or doors closing," Baker surmised. "So I can't imagine Ptown would be any different."

Jeffrey Doucette, a veteran ghost tour guide, said he's heard stories of table settings being rearranged and objects moving at Local 186 if guests or employees don't adhere to basic rules of etiquette. "I ran into one woman while I was giving the tour and she confirmed that the restaurant and inn's namesake was a bit of a stickler," said Doucette, adding that the former employee from Esther's Inn looked a little shell-shocked when he talked about the structure's alleged hauntings. "The spirit seems to be interested in table manners. The one woman who worked there said she used to scare the shit out of her. She didn't say if she was referring to the spirit or the former owner."

One theory as to why Local 186 is active is that the restaurant promotes spirit board sessions in its bar area. In fact, management boasts that they have "hot sauce for the dipping and a Ouija board for the chatting."

Joni Mayhan, author of the book *Ghostly Defenses: A Sensitive's Guide to Protection*, said it's dangerous for novices to play around with a Ouija. "I have mixed feelings about spirit boards, especially when they are used by inexperienced people," said Mayhan. "In some cases, it could be the equivalent of handing a loaded gun to a person who has never seen a gun before. The results could be fairly predictable."

Tara, a tour guide from Savannah, Georgia, told Mayhan that keeping a Ouija board around is trouble waiting to happen. "While she has witnessed professionals utilizing the board without issue, she's seen far more people get into trouble with them," reported Mayhan. "She believes that when inexperienced people use Ouija boards, hoping to sense a ghost or conjure their departed loved ones, other darker entities can come through instead, pretending to be the loved one."

Mayhan said she has heard of cases where spirit boards created a portal for darker entities to enter this world. However, she said it's possible to use the device as a tool to connect with the spirit world as long as it's used with caution. "They do work and will not bring any ill harm to you unless you believe that they will," she said. "What I recommend to others starting out is to respect the board and the spirits and no harm shall come. Never mock them and laugh at them."

So, is Local 186 haunted or is it just a case of a Ouija board session gone awry? Based on her personal experiences with spirit board sessions, Mayhan said it's possible that a bar patron has conjured up an evil entity.

"Using it can be a little more dangerous for the users since they have to allow the entity to use their bodies to control the planchette," Mayhan told *Paranormal Provincetown*. "I think any type of investigation inside an active location will certainly stir up the activity, especially if it's done too frequently and includes elements of provocation. If the ghosts are ornery to begin with, it only makes them meaner and more likely to lash out."

FILE UNDER *Wicked Ouija*

MARTIN HOUSE RESTAURANT

Built in 1750, this now-closed restaurant was supposedly a stop on the Underground Railroad and its hidden brick room, known as "snug harbor," allegedly hosts a family of spirits who cower in the corner. Also, patrons have spotted mysterious shadow figures reflected in mirrors and people claim that the third-floor loft boasts a malevolent poltergeist. "It used to be a restaurant and now it's a private residence, but I really want to get in there and investigate," explained Adam Berry. "A friend of mine who claims to be psychic said there are three entities in that house."

One ghost seems to be the spirit of Captain Tracy, who lived in the building in the 1700s. A misty outline of a sea captain has been seen in the upstairs dining room, accompanied by strange cold spots. The other ghosts may be the spirits of runaway slaves who sought shelter in the Martin House when it was part of the Underground Railroad. A small family of African American ghosts has been seen in a secret passage between two chimneys, while the ghost of a young slave girl has been reported to play pranks on people who sleep in the small upstairs room.

The classic, three-quarter Cape structure overlooks the Provincetown Harbor. It is believed that the couple who owned the building were involved in the abolitionist movement in the late 1800s. In addition to the secret "snug harbor" room, there's a second mystery spot on the third floor called the "secret room." In the early 1900s, it was owned by the Hatch family and used as a boarding house for Provincetown's elderly. By 1978, it was in a weathered state of disrepair. The Martin family purchased the historic structure in 1991 and turned it into a popular restaurant. It was during the 1990s when the owners reported a series of face-to-face encounters with the paranormal.

When the Martin House restaurant closed in 2005, after 30 years of operation, David Bowd and Kevin O'Shea purchased the building.

Michael Baker, a paranormal investigator with Para-Boston, told *Paranormal Provincetown* that the investigation his team led at Martin House in 2005 was inconclusive. "It was so noisy we had to discount all of our audio. There were two investigators at the time, no longer with the group, who claim to have seen shadows in the attic. They were not captured on tape unfortunately."

A science-driven expert, Baker said he goes into each investigation armed with a healthy dose of skepticism. "I think the place has some potential, but needs more efficient research," he continued. "I admit I was a bit skeptical having seen the owners' attitude toward the investigation of the property. I'm not convinced that even they believe it's haunted and may just be carrying forward the legend. Of course, this was in 2005 and things may have changed since then."

Built in 1750, this now-closed Martin House Restaurant was a stop on the Underground Railroad and its hidden brick room, known as "snug harbor," allegedly hosts a family of spirits who cower in the corner. *Photo by Sam Baltrusis.*

Baker said the Martin House's close proximity to the Provincetown Harbor may be a factor in its alleged activity. "Claims of hauntings and the sea are legendary and water may have played some component in legitimate activity, but I think there are also other elements missing such as more intricate formations of bedrock and the active fault lines that go along with it," he said. "That may keep activity in balance. It's hard to say."

When Dowd and O'Shea purchased the Martin House in 2005, it became residential property. According to a recent article in the *New York Times*, O'Shea said he and his partner haven't encountered the house's resident spirits. "The attic is where the ghosts are said to live," O'Shea explained. "Though we haven't seen sign of them yet."

While Baker and O'Shea aren't convinced, many believe the Martin House is one of Provincetown's most haunted sites. Mark Jasper, author of *Haunted Cape Cod & The Islands*, recounted some eerie tales from the crypt that suggested that the historic building is indeed haunted.

"The place is just chock-full of ghost stories," wrote Jasper. "Glen Martin believes that the ghosts that inhabit the Martin House come from this century as well as past centuries. His sister and a few other people have played witness to an apparition of a man who has appeared in nineteenth-century garb in one of the second-floor dining rooms."

According to Martin's account, there were also reports of ghostly activity on the first floor. "One woman told Glen that when she was a very young girl she remembered seeing a small man in that room while she was eating with her family," Jasper continued. "Now much older, the woman claims to see a convoluted mass of energy or ectoplasm. She believes the mass of energy is made up of different people who once lived in the house. The small man she first saw is thought to be one of the former owners, Mr. Hatch."

The most eerie close encounter happened in the fall of 1991. Martin was alone washing dishes in the kitchen and felt an eerie tap on his shoulder. He turned around and saw a man. He claimed it was a former owner of the Martin House and his name was John. According to Martin's account, the ghost of John was smiling at him but he slowly started to disappear. He said the ghost began "to fade away starting from the legs up until the only thing that remained was his head floating in mid-air...and then he vanished altogether," Martin told Jasper.

"Glen was in a state of disbelief and quite shaken by the incident," Jasper claimed. "Shortly thereafter, Glen received word that John had passed away that very same day."

Haunted House

CHAPTER 4

OVERNIGHT HAUNTS

Hotels where guests check in but don't check out? In Stephen King's *The Shining*, chef Dick Hallorann explained to the young Danny Torrance why the ghosts from the fictional Overlook Hotel continued to linger. "I don't know why, but it seems that all the bad things that ever happened here, there's little pieces of those things still laying around like fingernail clippings," he warned. Past traumatic events like murders and suicides can leave a supernatural imprint on a building, according to the telepathic chef.

When it comes to overnight haunts replete with paranormal residue, Provincetown isn't immune. Jeffrey Doucette, co-founder of the Haunted Ptown ghost tour, said the Outer Cape's most haunted have been turned into cozy bed and breakfast hideaways. "Provincetown is an old fishing community," he explained. "And when there's an old building with a weird historical backstory, there's potential for it to be haunted."

For example, Doucette has spent a lot of time crashing at the Provincetown Inn. Built in 1925, the West End haunt looks creepy. But is it haunted? "Every time I stay at the Ptown Inn, I expect the two girls from *The Shining* to show up," he mused. "But I haven't had a 'redrum' experience there yet."

However, he does think Ptown boasts a higher-than-usual percentage of haunted guest houses. Why? Doucette, who is a veteran tour guide in Boston, said there's a distinct difference between the haunted hotels near the Boston Common, like the Omni Parker House, and the overnight dwellings scattered throughout Provincetown. "What's interesting about Ptown is that a lot of the active old homes have been turned into guest houses. They weren't hotels or bed and breakfasts to begin with...they

Jeffrey Doucette said launching the Haunted Ptown tour in 2014 has given him a completely different perspective on the Outer Cape vacation spot. *Photo by Sam Baltrusis.*

Scene from the allegedly haunted corridor of the historic Provincetown Inn. *Photo by Sam Baltrusis.*

were homes," he said. "Provincetown's haunted corridor is Johnson Street with the Carpe Diem, Christopher's by the Bay and a slew of others around the corner."

The thirty-nine-year-old tour guide, who works in the finance department at a publishing house in Government Center when he's not moonlighting with Haunted Ptown, said he was raised in a superstitious Irish Catholic family. "My grandmother was a tinker, or an Irish gypsy, and she would go to confession and then she would read Tarot cards to make sure she was covering both ends of the spectrum," he joked. "I suspect a little of that tinker mysticism was passed on to me. My mother would always say people would die in threes. When someone passed, we made sure we left the windows open to let the spirits out."

Doucette was an amused skeptic until he gave his first Boston tour in 2009. "A kid on the tour shot a photo of me, and there were all of these white orbs near the Great Elm site," he explained. "The last photo really threw me for a loop. It was of me with a green light coming out of my belly, and I was freaked out." The tour guide said he reached out to a psychic who told him that the green light emanating from his torso was an indication that the spirits in the Boston Common liked the way he told their stories. "At the hanging elm, many of the people who were hanged there were done so unjustifiably by the Puritans for crimes they didn't commit. If anyone disagreed with the status quo at that time, they were executed. Boston was founded by Puritans, and it was either their way or the highway...or the hangman's noose."

Provincetown, in comparison, was where those who challenged the status quo would go to escape the Puritanical oppressors. Doucette said launching the Haunted Ptown tour has given him a completely different perspective on the Outer Cape vacation spot. "What I've learned from the tour is that Provincetown is more than a gay tourist destination," he continued. "You have 400 years of history with a vibrant maritime past. So much has happened on this tiny strip of land. Of course it's haunted."

Any surprises from the Provincetown tour? "There are gay ghosts," he said. "It's an LGBT enclave so it's to be expected. In other cities you don't have a ghost like Preston at the Rose & Crown. He was a drag queen and likes to make himself known during Carnival Week," Doucette explained. "If some drunk queen throws his wig on the ground, he's going to pick it up. Many spirits repeat behaviors that they did when they were alive. He was known to be a caretaker and it has continued into the afterlife."

So, what inn creeps out Doucette the most? "Carpe Diem, without a doubt," he shot back. "Oh, and the place where Tony 'Chop Chop' stayed, the Victoria House. I wouldn't be caught dead there."

CARPE DIEM

The literary-themed bed and breakfast known as Carpe Diem, located at 12 Johnson Street in Provincetown, is owned by partners Rainer Horn and Jürgen Herzog. It also had a past life as Provincetown's funeral home.

Dead poet's society? Yep, the inn is notoriously haunted. In fact, the William Shakespeare suite, room 9, is where guests sense an otherworldly presence, as if someone or something is standing behind them. In the Eugene O'Neill suite, workers have seen an imprint of a body on the bed when no one was in the room. There have also been reports of disembodied voices and shadow figures in the basement and a female apparition sporting black, turn-of-the-century clothing and walking down the stairs. It's no surprise that bodies were kept in the lower level, awaiting the embalming process and burial, in what was Provincetown's only funeral parlor.

One of the ghosts believed to haunt the inn is a former house manager who loved the property so much that he decided to stick around. Seize the day? Apparently, the Latin phrase is applicable even after they're six feet under.

Carpe Diem, located at 12 Johnson Street in Provincetown, is a literary-themed bed and breakfast and is notoriously haunted. *Photo by Sam Baltrusis.*

Two former employees, who wish to remain anonymous, told *Paranormal Provincetown* that the two-story, three-bay building is indeed active. "My first day on the job I heard footsteps coming up from downstairs and then a door slam," reported a former housekeeper. "I had no idea it was a funeral parlor. I asked 'is this place haunted?' and I was told that it was."

Jeffrey Doucette, tour guide with Haunted Ptown, said the Carpe Diem's ghost has a name. "Kevin is still there," Doucette confirmed. "Kevin was a manager and he apparently had a room downstairs. They called him the cellar dweller. He worked there for a long time. Anytime they're downstairs people report cold spots and footsteps going up the stairs. When they hear the phantom footsteps, they say it's Kevin."

Doucette said bodies were kept on ice in the carriage house at what is now the Carpe Diem. The structure, built in 1870, had a past life as the Trade Winds Inn. It's believed that Kevin managed the property during the pre-Carpe Diem era.

Mark Jasper, author of *Haunted Cape Cod*, interviewed the owners when the structure was newly renovated. He said a housekeeper reported a presence "as if someone was watching him or standing behind him."

Jasper also confirmed the ghostly shenanigans in the basement. "The same housekeeper mentioned that while in the basement he once heard someone talking in his ear and could actually feel someone's breath on the back of his neck. But when he turned around he could find no one." Another housekeeper reported seeing a mysterious figure walking into the room in the basement.

A woman who was in the hot tub where bodies were formerly kept on ice said she saw a man and a woman "dressed in weird clothes walking into the basement." The eyewitness said the couple were wearing garb dating back to the early 1900s. According to Jasper, "no one was ever found."

The ghostly woman, who is older and is wearing a black dress, is said to be a wailing woman spirit. She's upset and is walking to where the bodies were once kept. It's likely that someone she loved died there and she was paying her last respects. The lady in black is likely a residual haunting or a non-intelligent energy that somehow psychically imprinted itself into the historic building.

Guests have also reported haunted happenings in the Eugene O'Neill and Shakespeare rooms. One visitor claimed to see an imprint on his bed in the O'Neill suite. Others said that the door mysteriously unlocks, opens, and closes when no one else is there.

The Shakespeare room had a report from a woman who distinctly heard, "get up and get out," when she was in bed. No one else was in the room. Others claimed to have heard inexplicable noises and seen mysterious shadows in the room.

Jasper wrote about the rumors surrounding the Carpe Diem's cellar dweller, Kevin. "One of the ghosts is believed to be a former manager named Kevin who died years ago," wrote Jasper. "Apparently, he loved the inn so much his spirit is thought to have remained, looking after things. The identities of the other ghosts remain uncertain."

According to recent reports, activity at the house was exacerbated when the inn was under construction. "Paranormal activity seems to fluctuate at the Carpe Diem," continued Jasper. "At times, the guest house will become extremely active and then for unknown reasons things will quiet down."

Perhaps Kevin is taking a post-mortem vacation away from the inn he loved to death?

Cellar Dweller

CROWNE POINTE INN

What makes Provincetown's paranormally active inns unique? Compared to larger metropolitan areas replete with haunted hotels and spooktacular bed and breakfast spots, Ptown's overnight haunts are typically former homes.

Crowne Pointe Inn, located at 182 Bradford Street, is believed to be haunted by a sea captain who used to own the place. *Photo by Sam Baltrusis.*

In fact, many of the spirits allegedly lingering in the Outer Cape might be a byproduct of the strong-willed New England desire to maintain the old buildings of the past, which act as lures to both visitors and ghosts. "Spirits are attracted to the places they lived in," opined the late Jim McCabe, who was a noted ghost lore expert. "I think what attracts ghosts up here is that you don't tear down the buildings."

Crowne Pointe Historic Inn, located at 182 Bradford Street, is a 140-year-old restored estate that stands as an eerie sentinel on a hill. It has forty rooms and a resident, salty-dog spirit. The owners believe that a sea captain who used to own the place haunts their establishment.

Of course, Crowne Pointe Inn isn't the only haunted inn on the block with alleged paranormal activity.

CHRISTOPHER'S BY THE BAY

Christopher's by the Bay, located on Johnson Street, was built in 1843 for ship caulker Stephen Mott and his wife Eveline. The Victorian bed and breakfast boasts a female presence on the second floor. There are also reports of two children haunting the house while patrons in the guest rooms claim that books mysteriously fly off the shelves.

ATLANTIC LIGHT INN

At the Atlantic Light Inn, formerly called the Black Pearl Inn, located at 11 Pearl Street, it's said that at least two of the rooms in the 1830s-era inn are haunted. Animals refuse to enter room 6 and there are reports of a full-bodied apparition and inexplicable bloodstains in room 7. Zeke Cabal, who was known for his drunken shenanigans in the 1920s, is rumored to haunt the building and hide behind the corner desk in the inn's living room.

SHIREMAX INN

At the ShireMax Inn, located at 5 Tremont Street in the West End, guests have reported hearing phantom footsteps. They are believed to be those of a Vietnam War veteran of Portuguese descent who committed suicide by hanging himself in the building because of a broken heart. According to lore, he fell in love with an African-American woman and his family disapproved. Guests report hearing footsteps going down the stairs and the sound of the front door slamming when no one is around.

Crowne Pointe Inn got a makeover in 1999 and the new owners made a concerted effort to return the five-building structure, including the main house owned by the salty sea captain, to its original nineteenth-century glory. "The stately mansion that is now the main house of the Crowne Pointe Historic Inn was built near the turn of the nineteenth century for a prosperous sea captain of the Provincetown Harbor," the inn's website reported. "The grand carriage houses that stand behind the main residence, housed numerous fishermen once upon a time, were constructed shortly after."

Apparently, the sea captain liked how his former home was restored and continues to make a post-mortem return to his stately abode.

"A very old man believed to be the original inn's sea captain is seen pacing the hallways of the main inn," continued the website. "A ghostly image, often spotted on lobby surveillance cameras, shows a person wearing a flowing white robe, briskly strolling through the lobby late at

Christopher's by the Bay, located at 8 Johnson Street, was built in 1843 for ship caulker Stephen Mott and his wife Eveline. The Victorian bed and breakfast boasts a female presence on the second floor and two spirited children. *Photo by Sam Baltrusis.*

night. A heavy kitchen door that mysteriously opens in the evening and then closes again without human assistance."

Paranormal experts compare the ghosts at Crowne Pointe Inn to Boston's Omni Parker House. Why? Both hotels are supposedly haunted by their former owners.

Arguably the most haunted hotel in New England since opening its doors in October 1855, the Omni Parker House has been home to various sightings of the apparition of the hotel's founder, Harvey Parker, who reportedly has been spotted roaming the tenth-floor annex, checking up on unsuspecting guests. Other spooky happenings involve elevators mysteriously being called to the third floor—once frequented by both Charles Dickens and Henry Wadsworth Longfellow. That's also where the gender-bending lesbian actress, Charlotte Cushman, and an unnamed businessman died. In fact, one third-floor guestroom—yes, the mythic room 303—was supposedly converted into a closet after the unexplained reports of raucous laughter and the smell of whiskey spooked the management.

Like the marketing team at the Omni Parker House, staff at Crowne Pointe Inn have embraced the hotel's alleged ghostly inhabitants. In fact, Crowne Pointe Inn has posted a page on its website dedicated to ghost lore about an old-man specter keeping watch on his old home in the wee hours of the night. "Generations of guests and staff have regularly experienced events that would cause even the staunchest skeptic to take pause," the site mused. "Don't worry, all of our 'extra' visitors are friendly—so far."

FILE UNDER
Salty Specter

ROSE & CROWN

Built in the 1780s and one of the oldest homes in Provincetown, this Georgian-style "square rigger" is known for its eerie wooden-carved ship figurehead, nicknamed the Jane Elizabeth, who greets guests as they enter the guest house chock full of Victorian-era antiques and boasting a stunning front-yard garden.

Preston Babbitt, who owned the house in the '80s and passed away in the early '90s due to complications associated with HIV, is rumored to haunt the inn.

Babbitt loved the yearly Carnival parade and his spirit has been seen in the house wearing a white wedding gown, an outfit he wore proudly during the popular August street festival. Guests at the Rose & Crown have felt Babbitt's presence and have heard inexplicable noises coming from unoccupied rooms.

"Provincetown's welcoming gay-friendly reputation first attracted early AIDS victims to the Cape," wrote Ken Summers in *Queer Hauntings*.

Guests at the Rose & Crown have felt former owner Preston Babbitt's presence and have heard inexplicable noises coming from unoccupied rooms. *Photo by Sam Baltrusis.*

Built in the 1780s and one of the oldest homes in Provincetown, the Rose & Crown, located at 158 Commercial Street, is known for its eerie wooden-carved ship figurehead and its resident ghosts. *Photo by Sam Baltrusis.*

"Patients across the United States sought refuge from ostracism among its weathered clapboards."

Summers said Babbitt left an indelible mark on the community as an outspoken community activist and the former owner of the small inn. "Diagnosed as HIV-positive during the '80s, he knew too well the effects of the illness. Preston did his best to help those in need, yet found time for joy and laughter. His inn, located in an old Georgian from the 1780s, welcomed tourists in true Provincetown fashion. Preston would lounge in his front garden offering drinks and cheese to passersby."

Babbitt was president of the Provincetown Business Guild. However, it's his work during the AIDS crisis that is remembered most. "When people look back now at the time of AIDS in Provincetown, they mention how proud they are at how well the town rose to meet the crisis," penned Debra Lawless in *Provincetown Since World War II*. "In 1983, town nurse Alice Foley and others founded the Provincetown AIDS Support Group. With Babbitt, who owned the Rose & Crown Guest House, Foley made her rounds tending the desperately ill."

According to reports, Babbitt had a nurturing quality and made sure that "no one died alone." Some believe his mother-hen nature has continued in the afterlife.

Summers wrote about a close encounter of the paranormal kind with a ghost in drag at the Rose & Crown in 2000. A friend of the new owners spotted a mysterious figure in the rear innkeeper's quarters. "There, at the foot of the bed, stood a blue-eyed man with a pleasant face, dressed in a stark white wedding gown," continued Summers. "The house guest felt no fear and [the figure] faded into thin air after a few brief moments." The guest confirmed the identity of the spirit after spotting a painting "depicting the same blue-eyed fellow from the previous night." It was Babbitt.

What about the white dress Babbitt wore during Carnival? Summers explained that "Preston enjoyed dressing in drag. He often wore a particular wedding gown for the occasion, just as the ghost had appeared."

In addition to the inn's ghost in white, others claimed to have seen a shadow figure in the older part of the building called the Rose Room. "Visitors have reported a dark shadow figure walking through the chamber," the author wrote. "This is likely a different ghost, perhaps from another era of ownership. Or perhaps Preston has a spectral groom awaiting one final dance."

Visitors also claim that Babbitt's cat haunts the guesthouse, tiptoeing on beds in the wee hours of the night. "Though there are no animals currently on the premises (due to allergies), quilts in empty rooms indent as if a small creature has curled up on the covers," Summers claimed. "A few guests have reported the treading of paws walking up their beds in the night followed by a heaviness on their chests, approximately the same size and weight of a feline."

Joni Mayhan, a paranormal investigator and author, said sightings of ghost cats are common. "Pets who appear in ghost form haven't reincarnated yet and are simply returning to pay a visit to their grieving owners," Mayhan wrote in *Ghost Diaries*. "They will often give us subtle signs of their existence by exhibiting similar behavior to when they were alive. If your cat once knocked items off your counter, you very well might find objects in your house rearranged."

Mayhan told *Paranormal Provincetown* that it's possible that Babbitt's cat could have stayed behind to be with its owner in the afterlife.

Phantom puss in boots? Only in Provincetown.

Ghostly Drag

CHAPTER 5

SECRET HAUNTS

K nown as the spot where Pilgrims first set foot on Cape Cod on November 21, 1620, before signing the Mayflower Compact, it's no surprise that Provincetown is a town full of secrets and ghosts.

"After spending some time in Provincetown, one can come to feel that all of its time-honored public buildings and historic homes are loaded with ghosts," surmised *Cape Encounters*. "The eccentric quality of the town, its maritime location, the ramshackle layout of its structures, and its remote bittersweet atmosphere combine to create the impression of a hamlet permeated with supernatural energy."

Ashley Shakespeare, a veteran ghost tour guide and regular Provincetown drag illusionist, agrees. "Provincetown has always been Bohemian, artistic, and off the beaten path," he explained. "Spirits there, I feel, are the same way. While you may not know their names, you know they are there. Just like vacationers know that the kid who plays the piano at town hall will be there when they come back year after year. They don't know their names but know that they are there."

Shakespeare continued: "It's the same with the spirit world in Provincetown. They may not have any significant ties with any history or great events, but they are existing in their Bohemian, off-the-beaten-path world."

Ghosts with personalities? Shakespeare said his interactions with the spirit realm are similar to his encounters with the living. "You become friends with people because you understand them and they entertain you for various reasons. I feel spirits do the same thing," he said. "They make themselves known to people because they want fellowship."

Ashley Shakespeare, a veteran ghost tour guide, said the ghosts of Provincetown are more artistic and spirited compared to other New England haunts. *Photo by Ryan Miner.*

Shakespeare said he has been sensitive to the paranormal world for most of his life. He was raised in Manhattan and spent his formative years in Provincetown before moving to Revere. "Growing up, I always felt surrounded by a certain energy I couldn't explain and I knew most people couldn't or wouldn't understand it. I spent a lot of time alone as a child. I was very shy and wasn't involved in a lot of activities boys my age were. I often felt misunderstood, and I feel that the spirits that surrounded me felt the same way," Shakespeare remembered. "It hasn't changed much in my adult life except I'm more in tune with and have found a certain way to communicate with some spirits that want to make themselves known to me," he continued.

As far as communicating with the spirit realm, Shakespeare said he usually has a physical reaction when a ghost is nearby. "I get chills and goosebumps," he explained. "Every hair on my body stands up. I also have been physically touched by spirits and have seen them open doors, turn on TVs, and play with my pets."

Provincetown's most haunted? Shakespeare said the A-House and Route 6 because "many people have died on that road," adding that many decades ago "Long Point was the 'bad side of town' with pirates, gypsies, gambling and prostitutes," he explained. "With that cast of characters you can imagine the goings on that occurred. Also, there are a number of houses that were floated over from Long Point as the shorelines started to recede."

For the record, Long Point was a thriving village from 1818 through the late 1850s. Residents, mainly fishermen, who called the extreme tip of Cape Cod home, inexplicably decided to abandon the thin strip of land. One by one, they painstakingly floated their homes across the harbor. By the end of the Civil War, only two houses remained. The Long Point Light, built in 1827, stands as an eerie sentinel of what is now a ghost town. Historians are stumped as to what truly inspired the mass migration. Theories range from the lack of fresh water to proliferation of sharks.

However, Shakespeare believes the exodus was fueled by something more sinister.

He said the spirits from Long Point's nineteenth-century heyday continue to haunt the structures they once inhabited. "For the most part my relationships and interactions with the spirits in Ptown were the same as with those in the living world. We shared the same little town, glanced at each other as we went about our day," Shakespeare said, adding that there was one exception. "She was a mischievous eight-year-old girl. I lived in one of the floaters from Long Point in the West End on Atwood Lane."

Shakespeare believes the girl was killed, possibly crushed to death, when the house was moved to the West End.

"She was what you would think an eight-year-old little girl would be: inquisitive, mischievous and liked to play," he said. "She would unlock and open the kitchen door. I would wake up to find my TV on and the channel was changed to a station that I never knew I had, never mind watched. She also used to play with the cats and dog keeping them and herself entertained."

The former Provincetown year-rounder continued: "It was almost like having another little sister. I actually miss her sometimes and whenever I go to Ptown I walk by the house and say 'hello' to her."

Shakespeare said the spirits of Provincetown, including the mischievous ghost girl, don't creep him out. "The spirit world doesn't scare me," he responded. "Certain spirits may spook me from time to time, but I'm never scared. I've embraced the spirit world, and I feel once you embrace something, it doesn't scare you any longer."

His advice to visitors looking for a ghost adventure? "When in Ptown, go with the flow," he continued. "It's home to some and vacation paradise to others...both the living and the dead. Bask in the residual spirit energy... and consider it a gift to you from the ghosts of Provincetown."

EBEN HOUSE

Formerly known as the Fairbanks Inn, this historic structure located at 90 Bradford Street in the town's so-called haunted corridor, had a ghostly regular wearing eighteenth-century garb.

"This inn which dates back to 1775 was built by Eben Snow, a sea captain," reported *Cape Cod Online*. "It was later sold to David Fairbanks in 1826. He began the first Provincetown banking business in the front parlors of the building. Fairbanks would go on to establish the Seamen's Saving Bank and become the town's wealthiest resident. More recently, the inn began welcoming visitors in 1985."

The article confirmed the structure's ghostly connection, saying that "a Revolutionary War soldier is thought to haunt one of the 15 rooms at the Fairbanks Inn."

The website *Haunt Jaunts* pointed out the irony that the alleged ghost didn't appear to be one of the two former owners. "Interestingly, it's not a sea captain or banker whose ghost is reported to still roam here, it's a Revolutionary War soldier," *Haunt Jaunts* mused.

Why a Revolutionary War-era soldier ghost? For the record, Provincetown had a rather tumultuous history during the 1700s.

As the *Mayflower* Pilgrims quickly learned, Provincetown's geography makes it a natural bull's-eye. Its location at the end of one of the East

Eben's House, located at 90 Bradford Street, dates back to 1775 when it was called the Fairbanks Inn. It was built by sea captain Eben Snow. *Photo by Sam Baltrusis.*

Coast's longest peninsulas made it susceptible to repeated attacks and seizure. In fact, French brigades raided Provincetown's defenseless harbor after the early 1700s and depleted its human and commercial resources.

During the American Revolution, Provincetown contained 20 dwellings, 36 families, and 205 inhabitants. By 1790, it had a population of 454 people. During the Revolution, the British used Provincetown as a naval supply base for vessels, like the *Somerset*, which participated in the Battle of Bunker Hill and destroyed everything in its path, including the Boston Light, the beloved lighthouse on Little Brewster, which was built in 1716.

The *Somerset* sank on November 3, 1778, off Peaked Hill Bar, which was located near Provincetown's backshore.

Soldiers, some dressed in full redcoat regalia, swam ashore. It's estimated that 200 British regulars fleeing from the sunken *Somerset* died in the Provincetown Harbor. There are many reports of residual hauntings of British soldiers, including the mysterious sighting at Eben House, scattered throughout Provincetown. Paranormal investigators believe the residual hauntings, or a videotape replay of a tragic event, may be tied to the 200 soldiers who died in Provincetown's waters.

In 1776, "Captain Eben Snow finished building his house with wood taken from his vessel in the King's Navy," reported *Cape Encounters*. Before the inn's renovation as the posh Eben House, several employees reported that the office doorbell would ring mysteriously and seemed to have a mind of its own. "When the bell rings out of the blue, there is definitely nobody there," the book continued.

In addition to the Eben House's wood, which was swiped from the King's Navy, the Federal-style building also boasts a brick facade. It's one of three Federal-style buildings in Provincetown. Another notable brick home in the East End belonged to the late, great author Norman Mailer.

For years, the Bradford Street structure's claim to fame was its ties to the founder of Seamen's Savings Bank, David Fairbanks. In fact, a newspaper article from 1921 claimed that Fairbanks built the building himself for his family. The banker's mythic rise to fame as the town's wealthiest resident trumped Captain Snow's Revolutionary War-era mystique. Fairbanks was well liked.

To add to his likeability, there was a bank robbery in 1836 that generated national headlines. "One morning Mr. Fairbanks awoke to find that a large sum of money from his brick vault was gone as well as the clerk who lived with the family," reported the Provincetown Research Club. Knowing that the only way to escape Provincetown was by boat, Fairbanks' seafaring friends spotted a lone figure on a dory in the harbor. They waited until the clerk returned and figured out where the thief had hidden the cash. "The hiding place proved to be a cemetery close to a gravestone," continued the Research Club.

In the 1970s, the historic home was purchased by Stan Sorrentino who owned the Crown & Anchor. He turned it into a folk art museum. In 1985, the museum was converted into a guest house and it eventually became the Fairbanks Inn.

Recently, the new owners decided to pay homage to the building's founder and oddly the supposed hauntings stopped. "2015 marks a new chapter for this historic building, one of only three brick homes left from the colonial era in town," reported the structure's new owners. "Reopening as Eben House, and having undergone extensive restoration and modernization, the building (along with two others that have become part of the inn over the years) will set out to redefine bed and breakfast in Provincetown."

The centerpiece of the Salt Hotel's renovation is an artistic homage to Captain Eben Snow and his family. The large-scale portrait of Snow is a modern interpretation of eighteenth-century primitive portraiture painted by local artist Michael Gredier. Oddly, the artist's rendition of Snow looks a lot like the description of the full-bodied apparition of the Revolutionary War-era soldier spotted in the Fairbanks Inn.

Perhaps the spirit known to ring the bell at the old hotel was Snow himself demanding post-mortem recognition that he, in fact, built the glorious brick home on Bradford Street? Once the new owners honored the King's Navy sea captain, the ghostly doorbell stopped ringing.

 *Town Crier*

MACMILLAN WHARF

One if by land, "boo" if by sea? There have been legends of ghost boats and dories off the coast of Provincetown as long as sailors have set sail on its tumultuous waters.

Few ghost lore enthusiasts know this secret, but Provincetown was indirectly involved in a deadly close encounter with a so-called hoodoo ship at sea on March 6, 1869. During a torrential storm that eventually became a hurricane, a schooner known as the *Andrew Johnson* had a fatal collision with a vessel named the *Charles Haskell*. According to accounts from the *Haskell*, the schooner rammed into the *Andrew Johnson* during the hurricane and ripped it into pieces.

The *Johnson* was literally sliced open. The surviving ship's crew witnessed their peers frantically trying to stay alive. The vessel and its ten men were engulfed by the thrashing sea. They saw dark, shadowy figures rising out of the sea. There were ten of them in all, and as they reached the *Haskell*, the watchmen could see that the figures looked like men. The dark wraiths reached their hands over the rail of the schooner and climbed aboard. Their eyes were black, like hollowed-out holes, and they wore dark and oily seal skins for clothes. The phantoms quickly took up positions around the ship and began to go through the motions of casting lines, rigging sails, and setting the anchor.

After the ghostly encounter, the crew of the *Charles Haskell* abandoned the ship and it was found, years later, docked at Provincetown's MacMillan Wharf.

In 1974, there were several reports of a ghostly, three-masted frigate spotted in Boston Harbor and heading to Provincetown. A crew of Boston-based fishermen nearly ran into a vessel that paranormal enthusiasts jokingly call Boston's ghost guard.

"The fact that the sea mist was so mild made the crew's shock all the greater when they found themselves nearly crashing into a ship ahead of them," reported Joseph Mont in *Ghosts of Boston*. "This was no ordinary ship. The fishing vessel was a battered, barely seaworthy English frigate that appeared to be two centuries old. Not a man was seen on deck and not a soul was on the bridge."

According to Mont, the fishing boat's horn began to blast uncontrollably. "As the ship turned away from the frigate in retreat, the instruments all returned to normal," he wrote. "Then, as quickly as the frigate appeared, it vanished."

The phantom British boat, described as a wooden-hulled vessel with tattered sails and obvious battle scars, has been spotted from Boston to Provincetown. Witnesses who have seen the ghost frigate said it resembles

Provincetown was involved in a deadly close encounter at sea on March 6, 1869, with a so-called hoodoo ship named the *Charles Haskell*. The haunted *Haskell* was mysteriously found docked at Provincetown's MacMillan Wharf. *Photo by Sam Baltrusis.*

the USS *Constitution* in design but it's obviously British based on the discernable accents.

Witnesses have suggested the ghostly vessel could be the *Somerset*, which sank off the shore of Provincetown in 1778.

Or it could be the legendary *Flying Dutchman*. According to Tom Ogden's *Ghosts and Hauntings* book, it's probably the most commonly reported ghost boat. "Spotting the ancient vessel is supposed to be an omen of disaster," Ogden wrote. "Depending upon which version of the story you hear, the ship is supposedly cursed to sail for eternity without reaching port either because of a challenge of (or oath against) God or as some punishment for some sin."

The legend of the *Flying Dutchman* involved a specter that mysteriously appeared onboard. The boat's captain ordered the spirit to leave and when it didn't the captain pulled his pistol and shot at it. The mysterious specter then cursed the *Flying Dutchman*, saying: "And since it is your delight to torment sailors you shall torment them, for you shall be the evil spirit of the sea. Your ship shall bring misfortune to all who sight it." The spirit vanished and the *Flying Dutchman* sank, ultimately drowning the captain and all of the crew.

Of course, the *Flying Dutchman* is mere legend and has generally been spotted off South Africa's Cape of Good Hope. However, it could have made a detour to North America since it's doomed to sail the oceans for eternity.

Yes, even hell-ravaged ghost ships could benefit from a vacation in Provincetown.

And then there's the phantom dory. "It was first spotted in 1880 when a steamer, the *Nantucket*, tried to effect a rescue. But the boat disappeared," wrote Dennis Hauck in *Haunted Places*. "The dory is described as a black boat like those used for short-distance trawling. Sometimes it's surrounded by an eerie phosphorescence. Other times the bloodied body of a white man is seen in the bottom of the boat while a black man stands at the bow."

For years, Provincetown wasn't easily accessible because of its location at the extreme tip of Cape Cod. Because of its water-bound proximity, much of Provincetown's spooky maritime past has been lost at sea. However, a few ghostly tales have surfaced over the years, like long-forgotten messages in bottles, from Provincetown Harbor's frigid and apparently haunted waters.

Ghost Guard

Docked recently at Provincetown's MacMillan Wharf, the Oliver Hazard Perry is the first ocean-going, full-rigged ship to be built in the United States in more than a century. Its design resembles the cursed *Charles Haskell*. *Photo by Sam Baltrusis.*

PILGRIM MONUMENT

Built between 1907 and 1910 to commemorate the first landfall of the Pilgrims in 1620 and the signing in Provincetown Harbor of the Mayflower Compact, this 252-foot-tall structure is the tallest all-granite structure in the United States. The Pilgrim Monument was officially unveiled on August 5, 1910, after President Theodore Roosevelt laid the cornerstone in 1907. At the conclusion of the work there was great relief that not a single workman had been injured or lost his life during the construction.

However, there was one death related to the building of the Pilgrim Monument. It's of an elderly Provincetown lady called Rosilla Bangs.

In a strange accident, lightning struck one of the special rail cars that were used to transport the granite up High Pole Hill. The car broke loose from its fastenings and rolled rapidly down the hill toward a timber barrier that had been placed across the bottom of the hill in anticipation of an accident of this magnitude. The car was moving with such tremendous speed that it crashed through the barrier and across the street where eighty-five-year-old Bangs was standing on the sidewalk. She was paralyzed with fear.

Unfortunately, Bangs was directly in the path of the speeding rail car and was killed instantly.

The woman has since been spotted sitting on that bench on Bradford Street. Some say she's a "stay behind," a type of spirit that doesn't know she's dead due to the bizarre circumstances in which she died. The late Dr. Hans Holzer, in an interview in 2005, explained the phenomenon. "'Stay behinds' are relatively common," he said. "Somebody dies, and then they're really surprised that all of a sudden they're not dead. They're alive like they were. They don't understand it because they weren't prepared for it. So they go back to what they knew most—their chair, their room, and they just sit there. Next, they want to let people know that they're still 'alive.' So they'll do little things like moving things, appear to relatives, pushing objects, poltergeist phenomena, and so on."

It's believed that Bangs attached herself to the bench on Bradford and has been waiting for the trolley for more than 100 years.

In addition to the haunted bench on Bradford Street, there's a former inn turned private home located at Six Webster Place that's also a stone's throw from the Pilgrim Monument. The three-quarter Cape was empty for years before it was purchased in the mid-1980s. During renovations of the creepy cottage, one of the owners decided to move several gravestones impeding the building's foundation.

Not a good idea. As soon as the man identified in the book *Cape Encounters* as Mario Lebert moved the markers he started hearing phantom footsteps.

In a strange accident during the making of the Pilgrim Monument, lightning struck one of the rail cars that was used to transport the granite up High Pole Hill and fatally crushed 85-year-old Rosilla Bangs. *Courtesy Boston Public Library, Print Department.*

Killed during a freakish accident during the making of the Pilgrim Monument, Rosilla Bangs is believed to have psychically attached herself to the bench on Bradford Street and has been waiting for the trolley for more than 100 years. *Photo by Sam Baltrusis.*

Apparently, he used a gravestone to plug up a hole in the foundation. It was when the former owner blocked the opening that all hell broke loose.

"When I was working on the house, I used to hear them upstairs," Lebert recalled. "I'd go upstairs, figuring it was my partner, but he was gone."

The owner, a noted skeptic, said he heard the creepy footsteps for six weeks. A neighbor pointed out that Six Webster Place was notoriously haunted and was featured in the *Boston Herald* in the 1930s. The story mentioned a mischievous poltergeist as well as "noises and crying from beyond."

Lebert immediately returned the gravestones to their original location and the hauntings mysteriously stopped. "I really didn't give any thought to the noises," Lebert told *Cape Encounters*. "They didn't scare me."

David Dunlap's *Building Provincetown* also mentions the ghost lore associated with the Webster Place structure. According to Dunlap, there was a headline in the December 1936 *Provincetown Advocate* claiming that Six Webster Place was a "Haunted House Damaged By Fire." A woman named Minerva Perry, obviously unfazed by the ghostly rumors, purchased the building in 1937. The so-called haunted house was vacant for 24 years after

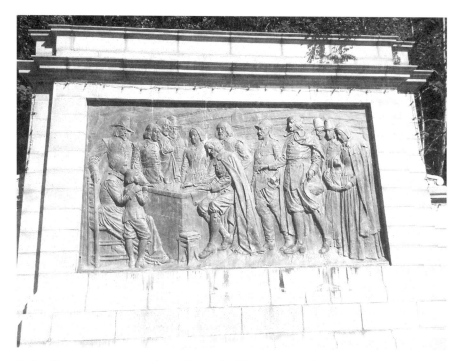

Sculpted in 1929, this granite sculpture depicts the Pilgrims signing the Mayflower Compact. *Photo by Sam Baltrusis.*

Perry's death. It was later turned into a bed and breakfast from 1987 to 1997.

Of course, it could be Six Webster Place's sentinel spirit. "The motif of the haunted house is a deep-rooted one, perhaps having its origin in the ancient belief that each place, including dwellings, had its own 'genuis loci,' which in Roman mythology meant the protective deity/spirit of a location, but which could be the place's distinctive spirit," wrote Brian Haughton in *Lore of the Ghost.*

Christopher Duff and Mark A. Westman purchased Six Webster Place in 2005, and it returned to its roots as a private home. Westman told Dunlap that the foundation of the home, which included hand-hewn floor joists, dates as far back as the mid-eighteenth century. However, the building first appeared on Provincetown maps in 1858. Known previous owners included G. Snow in 1880 and W. Smith in 1907.

Duff and Westman were warned to leave the gaping hole next to the base of the chimney alone. Apparently, the breach in the basement acted as a portal of sorts for the spirit world. "Our contractor told us, 'Whatever you do, don't close up the opening,'" Westman informed Dunlap. "'That's where the spirits come and go.'"

Six Webster Place was empty for years before it was purchased in the mid-1980s. Former owners claimed that the hole in the foundation is a ghostly portal. *Photo by Sam Baltrusis.*

Pilgrim's Phantoms

VIOLA COOK

Known as Provincetown's "sail away lady," Viola Cook's mental breakdown aboard the whaler *Bowhead* after six winters at sea north of the Arctic Circle with only her domineering husband for company is Provincetown legend. She died November 20, 1922, in her home, at the site of the present-day Womencrafts at 376 Commercial Street. However, it's said that the remarkable woman's pioneering spirit lingers in the afterlife.

"Some have referred to Viola Cook as the tragic victim of a relentless Arctic winter where she was driven mad by isolation and her husband's almost maniacal quest to fill his ship with whale oil and bone," reported Jim Coogan in *Sail Away Ladies*. "Years after her final experience in the Arctic, people in Provincetown remembered her as a crazy old lady who cursed like a sailor and talked to herself as she walked along Commercial Street."

Coogan said she exhibited psychotic behaviors after returning to Provincetown, degrading mentally each return trip while enduring six winters at sea. "There were some who whispered of hearing strange singing coming from her house in the middle of the night and of her reported habit of constantly sharpening long kitchen knives during the day," Coogan penned.

The singing stopped when she died of heart failure in her Commercial Street home in 1922.

"Viola Cook's death was in keeping with the stark tragedy of her life," wrote Mary Heaton Vorse in *Time and the Town*. "Neighbors noticed that no smoke had come from her chimney for a day or two, and when they broke in they found her on the bathroom floor, where she had died of heart failure."

According to multiple sources, Cook became an invalid the last few years of her life. Her depression was so severe that her husband, who passed away sixteen years later in 1938, filed for divorce and married a younger woman who was thirty-eight. The "sail away lady" of Commercial Street died six days after her husband left Provincetown to start a citrus business in Florida.

"What Mrs. Cook may have seen of brutality, she wouldn't admit into her consciousness," continued Vorse in *Time and the Town*. "She would be seen in her yard, brushing out the Captain's clothes when he was expected back. Especially disturbed was she at the full of the moon, and one could hear her wailing hymns at such times. The story is, too, that when Captain John Cook came home he pushed heavy furniture beside the door of his room because Mrs. Cook had the habit of honing the kitchen knives razor-sharp, as the knives of a whaling vessel are kept."

Dead end? Provincetown's Viola Cook is said to haunt the area around her former home, currently Womencrafts at 376 Commercial Street. *Photo by Sam Baltrusis.*

What happened at sea? Cook told the *Boston Globe* that it was extremely isolated and that "sewing helps to dispel the monotony that will manifest itself assertively at times." She described her sixth "wintering over" as unbearable. "One would suppose the voyager would need to hug the fire to avoid perishing when I tell you that the temperature was as low as fifty-seven below zero, and for weeks never rose above fifty during our winter at Baille Island," Cook told the *Boston Globe*.

The last few trips to the Arctic seem to be what pushed Cook over the edge. She initially refused to go during the summer of 1902. Her husband, unhappy with the decision, took a train to San Francisco without her. Cook ended up joining her husband and their journey continued through 1905. According to Coogan, she told her husband that "she would rather die than spend another season locked in the cold and icy darkness."

She survived the winter of 1905 but not mentally. It's said she returned to San Francisco in the summer of 1906 a broken woman. "Her contentment and vivacity fled, giving place to despondency," her husband wrote in his memoir called *Thar She Blows* after her death. "The disappointment fairly overwhelmed her. So completely was she prostrated by grief, her nervous system was shattered and she eventually sank in melancholia."

Captain Cook coerced his wife to return in 1910. He had a new whaler built for her final journey. He called it the *Viola* in her honor. However, the woman's sanity was far gone at this point. Cook's marbles were literally lost at sea.

The woman's post-traumatic insanity was immortalized in Eugene O'Neill's 1917 play *Ile*. "His portrayal had her playing the piano wildly in the darkened cabin of her frozen whaleship, her mind disintegrating while her Ahab-like husband blindly pursued his ghostly whales," Coogan described in *Sail Away Ladies*.

Four years before Cook's death in 1922, the vessel called *Viola* mysteriously disappeared at sea. Captain Cook sold it to his daughter Emma's husband, Captain Joseph Luis. All on board the *Viola* perished in 1918. It's believed that Cook's namesake brig was destroyed by a German submarine.

As far as the intrepid woman's spirit is concerned, people around Cook's former home on Commercial Street report disembodied singing in a haggard female voice, rocking chairs mysteriously moving on their own and an occasional howl at the full moon from the crazy lady's old haunt next to Pearl Street. Is it Cook? Some locals believe it's Provincetown's "sail away lady" making a postmortem plea, begging her husband to return home before the icy Arctic waters freeze over.

FILE UNDER

Dead End

CHAPTER 6

TRURO HAUNTS

Peter Muise, author of *Legends and Lore of the North Shore* and founder of the blog *New England Folklore*, said there's something mysterious and oddly enchanting about Provincetown's Outer Cape neighbor, Truro.

"The whole area does feel magical to me," said Muise. "I think it's the combination of the woods, the ocean, and the big, wide-open sky. A huge part of it is protected as the Cape Cod National Seashore. It's very different from other parts of New England."

When the English Pilgrims first visited in 1620 before signing the Mayflower Compact, Truro was populated with the Wampanoag tribe. As legend suggested, the Pilgrims made a sojourn for supplies and scoured Provincetown and Truro. They stumbled upon some fields cleared for farming and a stash of much-needed food known as Corn Hill in Truro.

The Pilgrims allegedly stole supplies from the Wampanoag tribe and kept them in a metal kettle that looked as though it came from Europe. That corn was literally a life saver. Roughly ten bushels provided a crop for the spring and was a much-needed food source after a winter that killed a large percentage of the men and women who fled to America seeking religious freedom.

So, the successful colonization of Massachusetts may have started with an act of larceny.

"Truro is very old," continued Muise. "It was one of the first places the Pilgrims stopped when they arrived in North America, and of course was inhabited by Native Americans for thousands of years before that. The Pilgrims supposedly stopped by a spring in Truro to get fresh water

Peter Muise, author of Legends and Lore of the North Shore, said that Provincetown's neighbor Truro is indeed creepy and possibly haunted. *Photo by Sam Baltrusis.*

and they also may have stolen some Wampanoag corn at Corn Hill."

Similar to its Cape Cod neighbor, Truro and North Truro are hotspots for legend and lore. In fact, the local stories involving seventeenth-century accusations of witchcraft echo similar tales including so-called "spectral evidence" circulating in nearby cities like Salem and Boston.

"One tells how a sea-captain named Sylvanus Rich was sailing past Truro when he sighted a small hut on one of the Atlantic beaches," explained Muise. "He rowed ashore and purchased some milk from the old woman inside. He returned to his ship, but after drinking the milk fell under the old woman's power. She appeared to him every night when he slept, put a bridle in his mouth, and rode his spirit up and down the Cape like a horse. Every morning he awoke exhausted. His crew was skeptical of his story until he showed them the spur marks on his side. He grew weaker and weaker, until his son arrived on a passing ship and broke the spell. Unfortunately, the legend doesn't specify how he did this."

Also, like the Black Flash in Provincetown, Truro had its very own cryptid known as the "Beast of Truro."

According to Muise, the catlike animal has been spotted as recently as 1981. "Three pigs were found slaughtered in their pens. About a dozen house cats were killed. An animal very similar to a mountain lion was seen by a local couple and a tourist from New York," Muise said. "The Truro couple thought that cat weighed about eighty pounds and had a long tail. The authorities were never able to find it and the animal killings stopped just as suddenly as they had begun."

Monsters in Truro? Muise said the National Seashore landscape is fertile ground for tall tale legends. "Truro has a lot empty space and

The Pilgrims allegedly stole supplies from the Wampanoag tribe and kept them in a metal kettle. That corn was literally a life saver. *Courtesy Boston Public Library, Print Department.*

conservation land, so I can understand why people would think a big predator like this might be hiding somewhere," he continued.

And, of course, there's Truro's haunted history. Muise said the town's Native American past is a major player in its ghost lore. "A lot of the Native American lore from this area was lost, but the original inhabitants of Truro would have had a much different relationship to the spirit world than the Pilgrims or modern Americans," Muise said.

"Ghosts and nature spirits were accepted as part of the world. People now are either fearful or skeptical of ghosts and spirits, but I think the Wampanoag would have seen them as part of the natural order that should be treated with respect," he continued. "There were rules for dealing with those types of entities and I think people today have forgotten what those rules are."

Although the summer vacation community is a stone's throw from Provincetown, Muise said the two towns are worlds apart, mainly due to Truro's off-season "ghost town" vibe. "Truro is much quieter, but of course Ptown has its quiet spots as well," Muise responded. "Still, you can walk on some of the beaches in Truro and not see another person, even in the summer. Some people might find that spooky but I think it's great. Truro is more meditative. Ptown is more social. Truro has more nature. Ptown has more culture."

So, what specifically spooks Muise about Truro? "There aren't any places that creep me out, but there are times that creep me out," he said. "Walking on some of the big empty beaches after dark? Kind of creepy. It feels like you are going back to a more primitive, primal era. It's just you and whatever is out there in the dark."

JENNY LIND TOWER

Yes, Truro has its very own haunted medieval-style structure. It's known as the Jenny Lind Tower and the story behind this creepy structure is almost as bizarre as the ghost lore associated with it.

Peter Muise, the writer behind the popular *New England Folklore* blog, said he tried to make the trek out to the tower a few years ago but was deterred by the threat of ticks and other creepy crawlers. "If you visit the Highland Light you'll get a great view of the landscape. Off in the distance you can see an Air Force Radar dome, and next to it what looks like the tower from a medieval castle. This is the Jenny Lind Tower."

Lind, also known as Johanna Maria Lind, was a famous nineteenth-century Swedish opera singer, explained Muise. Circus impresario P. T. Barnum arranged for "The Swedish Nightingale" to tour the United States in the 1850s and enormous crowds turned out to see her perform in every city. Her Boston performance was booked at a large train station (one of the few venues big enough to accommodate the estimated audience), but the promoter oversold the tickets and hundreds of people weren't able to get in.

According to Muise, the people who couldn't get into the concert became angry and started rioting. Windows were smashed and doors were ripped off their hinges. To calm things down, Lind ascended one of the train station's towers and serenaded the rioting mob. As soon as they heard her powerful soprano voice the crowd was entranced and became peaceful. The tower she sang from became known as the Jenny Lind Tower.

"In the 1920s the train station was dismantled. A lawyer named Henry Aldrich bought the tower and moved it to its current Truro location, where he had some summer cottages," Muise continued. "Tradition says that he bought it because he was a big Lind fan, but that may not be true. Eventually his family gave the land and the tower to the Cape Cod National Seashore."

Aldrich wasn't even born when Lind gave her legendary outdoor concert. Experts like Muise say we may never know why Aldrich moved the tower and had crews reconstruct it brick-by-brick on the barren hillside of North Truro. For the record, the seventy-foot tower is solid granite and lined with bricks.

With such a mysterious backstory, the Jenny Lind Tower is also notoriously enchanted. According to *Cape Cod Online*, there remains a "haunting beauty" to the legend. "It is speculated that Jenny Lind still resides in the tower and, on a summer's evening, visitors can hear the lifting sound of her melodies serenading them over the dunes."

Muise confirmed that Lind's ghost can supposedly still be heard singing from the structure. And, oddly, her lingering energy is a bit of a snob when it comes to modern-day tunes. "It's said that her spirit doesn't like contemporary music, so if you make your way to the tower, be respectful," warned Muise. "I'm not sure why her ghost would haunt the tower."

Perhaps it's just a psychic imprint or post-mortem echo of a powerful event from the building's past.

"When I first learned about the tower in 2008, I asked some local residents for directions to it," recalled Muise. "At the time I was told two things. First, that no roads lead to it and second, that I would become covered in ticks if I tried to bushwhack my way there."

Muise joked that Lyme's disease is scarier than ghosts, so he decided not to risk it. "I don't think the situation has changed much recently," he said. "Getting to the tower could be dangerous to your health."

The tower has been off-limits to paranormal investigators because of its hard-to-reach proximity and the fact that it's situated on land that was deeded to the Cape Cod National Seashore by a relative of Aldrich in 1961. "You can't get to the tower without trespassing on private land," wrote Bruce Gellerman

In 1927, a local businessman moved the allegedly haunted Jenny Lind Tower from Boston to North Truro. According to Peter Muise, the tower is haunted by Lind's ghost and she reportedly disapproves of modern music. *Photo by Sam Baltrusis.*

and Erik Sherman in *Massachusetts: Quirky Characters, Roadside Oddities and Other Offbeat Stuff.* "But you can drive up Highland Road and park at the Highland Light Beach parking lot to take a look and a bow."

While it's nearly impossible to get up close and personal to the Jenny Lind Tower, Muise hopes visitors will have access to the allegedly haunted structure in North Truro.

"The Jenny Lind Tower is very close to an abandoned Air Force base that is being developed as a cultural center, called the Highland Center," he explained. "Hopefully the tower will be incorporated into the center so visitors can access it more safely. Maybe Jenny's ghost will get a new audience after all these years."

 *Dark Tower*

PHANTOM TRAINS

North Truro can be downright creepy, especially at night. Some believe it's related to the Native American energy still lingering in the sandy brush while others think it's tied to the odd amount of maritime-related deaths occurring off the less-populated Outer Cape tourist destination. "When I go camping in North Truro, I can feel the presence of the ghosts of shipwrecked passengers," remarked one visitor to the Provincetown Paranormal Research Society's (PPRS) Facebook page. "I ask God to bless them so they can be at peace and cross over to heaven."

And then there's the recurring reports of a phantom train chug-chugging along to its final destination in Provincetown. "I've heard it in North Truro, on Shore Road, on more than one occasion," commented another visitor to PPRS's site. "It's always clearly a train. I keep thinking it's some sort of feedback loop from when the trains came to the ice house at Cold Storage Beach. But who knows?"

Another local, Jeremy, confirmed the online phantom train chatter. "I have heard it down behind Shore Road just down the hill from Terra Luna restaurant," he wrote. "It's always traveling in the same direction, heading toward Provincetown. Usually I would hear them between 9:30 p.m. and 11 p.m."

Peter Muise, author of *Legends and Lore of the North Shore*, said he has no clue why multiple locals in North Truro report hearing a ghost train. Could it be a psychic imprint from the town's diesel-engine past? "That's kind of creepy, but I have no clue," responded Muise. "I haven't read or heard anything about a train disaster in Truro. Trains used to run all the way out to Provincetown but haven't for at least fifty years."

Skeptic Michael Baker from Para-Boston said it's a "familiar tale along abandoned train lines," adding that it's a somewhat clear case of the power of suggestion. "I know the Hoosac Tunnel in western Massachusetts also has claims like that as well. Even *Ghostbusters II* made reference to phantom trains on the old pneumatic transit system thus showing its impact on popular legends," he explained. "Some claims may be due to suggestion. The knowledge of tracks and an old train can induce correlated hallucinations."

Baker continued: "If the phenomena is authentic and recordable it may be residual and support the idea of audible instances recording within the environment. That element itself is something that certainly requires further research. It's a difficult subject to wrap a scientific approach around."

For the record, the Cape's first train passed through North Truro on July 23, 1873. The Old Colony Railroad Line was extended starting from Wellfleet and ending on Provincetown's Bradford Street between Alden and Standish. The premiere journey was a big deal, attracting local dignitaries and crowds

All aboard? Locals report hearing phantom trains in North Truro even though the last ride to Provincetown occurred more than fifty years ago. The Railroad Avenue sign in Provincetown marks the long-gone locomotive's final destination. *Photo by Sam Baltrusis.*

of revelers on High Pole Hill. After the trains had been running for sixty-five years, the last passenger train trekked through the tip of the cape's sandy terrain on July 1938. Freight trains continued until 1960 with four stops in Truro including Corn Hill and North Truro Railroad Station, which is located at the intersection of Pond and Twinefield Roads. The tracks were dismantled from Eastham to Provincetown more than fifty years ago.

However, locals insist that the ghostly choo-choo is a residual haunting or a videotaped playback of past events, creeping through North Truro late at night.

"It sounds like a real train to me, too," added another local on the PPRS page. "The house I grew up in was within earshot of a train track so it's been a comforting sound to hear it."

Tom Ogden wrote about the railway-phantom motif in *Ghosts and Hauntings*. "Ghosts and phantoms have been reported on trains and along railroad tracks for as long as there has been an Iron Horse," Ogden opined. "Collisions and derailments were a regular part of train travel," he explained, adding that "there's a whole genre of ghost lights that haunt railways."

Of course, the most celebrated locomotive ghost is Abraham Lincoln's funeral train, which made the journey from Washington, DC, to Springfield, Illinois, in 1865. Odgen said people continue to encounter the former president's black-draped funeral train generally around the anniversary of Lincoln's assassination on April 15. "Many people living along the rail line claim to see the funeral train pass by," Ogden penned. "The train is always described as being black and some imaginative percipients see a crew of skeletons."

The eerie sounds of North Truro's ghost train continue to be a mystery. Some believe the inexplicable noise is a foghorn from the Wood End lighthouse. Others suggested on the *Provincetown Community Space* that it's a machine the town uses to paint the crosswalks overnight.

One woman, formerly from New Hampshire, said she had no clue the town's train station had long been razed. "For the record, I've heard the train here in North Truro," she chimed in on the conversation. "I lived near the tracks in New Hampshire for so long that the first time I heard it down here it didn't even occur to me that there is no train down here. I've only heard it in the winter," she surmised, concluding that sound travels better during North Truro's desolate colder months.

FILE UNDER

Phantom Menace

SALTY MARKET

Close encounters with UFOs and ghost lore rarely overlap. However, it's hard to overlook North Truro's history of unidentified flying objects. In fact, the former Highland Road location of Dutra's Market, recently renamed Salty Market, was the site of one of Cape Cod's more infamous alien abduction cases.

Robert Matthews shared with the popular TV show *Unsolved Mysteries* in 1988 about a phenomenon known as "missing time." According to his account, an Air Force officer disappeared for an hour after being dropped off at Dutra's Market. Under hypnosis, he related what he later described as an abduction by alien spacecraft.

It was 8:45 p.m. on October 1, 1966. Matthews was 19 at the time and he was reporting to his first tour of duty as a first class airman. He was on a bus and was dropped off at the deserted Dutra's Market. What happened next would change Matthews's life forever.

"I got off where the bus driver told me where I was supposed to get off," Matthews told *Unsolved Mysteries*. "And he told me to phone the base and they would send a truck down to pick me up. I told him that I was in front of Dutra's Market and he told me to stay there and that there would be a truck there to pick me up in a minute. While I was standing there, I saw these lights you know, moving from right to left across the sky. That's when I felt this fear."

According to reports, the Air Force truck tried to retrieve the new recruit five minutes after the initial call. Matthews did call a second time but it was recorded almost an hour later at 9:45 p.m.

"When I called the base again, they asked me where I'd been and he told me, he says, we sent a truck down there already. And I say, well I've been standing here waiting and no one's been by here."

The phenomenon known as "missing time" became a passion for the recently deceased author Budd Hopkins. The two men met up and Hopkins told *Unsolved Mysteries* that Matthews possibly had a close encounter with a UFO during his hour-long memory lapse.

"It is not perceived as a break in which something happens and then a resumption. It is...remembered as continuous and...the half-hour trip...turns out to be a two-hour trip or whatever, and this is sometimes experienced in conjunction with a UFO sighting or something like a light, but not always," explained Hopkins, who went on to write bestselling books including *Witnessed* and *Intruders*.

During hypnosis, Matthews was able to recall what happened to him outside of Dutra's Market in North Truro.

Salty Market, formerly called Dutra's Market, was the site of one of the Outer Cape's more notorious reports of an alien abduction which involved Robert Matthews. *Photo by Sam Baltrusis.*

"Under hypnosis, I observed in the sky, three lights moving in this direction. They hovered over here," Matthews told *Unsolved Mysteries* outside the market. "And the red one came at me so fast. I walked up to the ramp and I looked inside. And I saw four beings sitting. The place reminded me of a doctor's office."

According to *Provincetown Magazine*, North Truro became a hotbed of alleged UFO sightings once the TV show aired in the late '80s. "The recollections of the late Matthews are transcribed from a 1988 episode of the television show *Unsolved Mysteries*, which featured his story as well as Hopkins, and put North Truro on the map for UFO believers and skeptics alike," the magazine reported.

The article, published in 2011, featured a group called MUFON or the Mutual UFO Network, which was spearheaded by astrologer Carolyn Miller. "Most everyone who has lived on Pond Road has reported seeing some really strange things," said Miller of the area near North Truro, which appears to be a hotspot for alien visitation. "Just recently someone saw lights hovering over the old church there."

Hopkins, who vacationed regularly in North Truro, became an expert on "missing time," in addition to being a successful abstract expressionist artist in NYC, before his death in 2011. "Over years of interviews, Hopkins came to the conclusion that aliens were experimenting with the sexual biology of their human subjects in an attempt to strengthen their own gene pool, which he believed had become depleted," reported the *Barnstable Patriot* in Hopkins's obituary. "He referred to abductees as 'victims' because they were unwilling test subjects in these scary medical procedures and felt that nothing positive could come from these alien encounters."

FILE UNDER

Space Invaders

CONCLUSION

When I write my historical-based books, I spend months and sometimes years researching the ghost lore associated with a city or town before I even pitch the book to my publisher. I also let the "ghosts" guide me, so I allow my intuition to summon me to the sites covered in the book at first. Sometimes my gut leads me into extremely scary situations, which was the case with my last book, *Ghosts of Salem: Haunts of the Witch City*.

Provincetown? It's a different kind of creepy.

My experience writing *Paranormal Provincetown* was completely different compared to crafting my last book. "Provincetown is equally as haunted as Salem, but the spirits aren't as pissed off," I told Solaris BlueRaven on her weekly podcast, *Ravenstar's Witching Hour*. "There's dark contemporary history in Provincetown compared to Salem. It was a playground for serial killers, mobsters and underground activity from the '50s to the '70s. It's literally the tip of the world. It's the eastern-most point of Cape Cod so it has an end-of-the-world vibe to it. People who want to get away gravitate to Provincetown. A lot of creative types, like Tennessee Williams and Eugene O'Neill, went there to be inspired. It has beautiful beaches and its overall vibe is magical…but it's also very haunted."

I talked about how ghost lore was part of the vernacular of Salem. In Provincetown, year-round locals admit that the town is extremely active with spirits, but they are wary to go on the record and give the lowdown about their ghostly encounters. "What happens in Provincetown stays in Provincetown and that's the case with its ghost lore as well," I joked on BlueRaven's radio show.

If you're looking for ghosts, it's best to visit Provincetown during the off-peak season, which is September through December. October is my favorite time for an extended stay at the LGBT-friendly tourist destination. In fact, former Police Chief Jeff Jaran estimated that Ptown has become the second largest Halloween gathering in the state after, no surprise, Salem.

Here's a historical timeline of events highlighting Provincetown's dark, 400-year history. The information was pulled from a well-researched document from the town's official website (www.provincetown-ma.gov/DocumentCenter/Home/View/874).

1602

Bartholomew Gosnold, an English seafarer, explored and mapped the Cape on board his vessel the *Concord*. James Brereton chronicled the journey and wrote about the would-be colonists contact with the Native American Wampanoag tribe. The *Concord* returned to England armed with a boat full of sassafras. Gosnold is the first to call the land Cape Cod.

1614

Captain John Smith explored Cape Cod and met the Indian princess Pocahontas during his journey to collect fish and furs. Charts from Smith's era referred to Cape Cod as Cape James, after the British king. Provincetown Harbor was called Cape Cod Harbor.

1619

Explorer Thomas Dermer found the Cape's Native population decimated by disease contracted by the previous English visitors.

1620

The *Mayflower*, armed 101 passengers from England seeking religious freedom, dock off the backshore of Provincetown near Long Point in November 1620.

1620

The Mayflower Compact was signed in the Provincetown Harbor on November 11, 1620. The Pilgrims spend five weeks exploring the tip of Cape Cod and ventured as far as Eastham, where they had their first encounter with the Native American population. Dorothy May Bradford, leader William Bradford's wife, fell overboard and drowned on December 10 and Peregrine White became the first colonist child born in the New World on December 16.

1621

The colonists transfer to Plymouth and at least half of the passengers died of disease and hunger before the spring. A second group of colonists aboard the *Fortune* arrive in Provincetown Harbor and were shocked to see that no one had settled on Cape Cod.

1623

The group of Native Americans who first encountered the Mayflower Pilgrims were the Pamets. The group's sachem, Massasoit, created a federation of tribes known as the Wampanogs.

1630

The Puritans, also seeking religious freedom, settle Boston and form the Massachusetts Bay Colony.

1654

Governor Thomas Prence of the Plymouth Colony purchases the lands at the tip of the Cape, known as the Province Lands, from the Chief of the Nausets.

1661

Chief of the Nausets sold the Province Lands to Governor Thomas Prince, as representative of the Plymouth Colony. The selling price was two brass kettles, six coats, twelve axes, twelve knives and a box. The purchase included land from Eastham to Provincetown's Long Point.

1680

Provincetown developed a bad reputation attracting troublemakers who created fishermen's shacks on the beach. The motley crew included outlaws, smugglers, heavy drinkers and "Mooncussers" who would lure ships to their doom by placing lighted lanterns on the beach at night, thus forcing ships to wreck on sandbars offshore and then salvaging the goods.

1696

Ephriam Doan is said to be the first recorded birth in what will become Provincetown.

1714

Truro, which was incorporated in 1709, was given jurisdiction over the tip of Cape Cod.

1719

A sea monster was reported in the Provincetown Harbor by B. Franklin, the uncle of the famous Benjamin Franklin. According to Franklin's account, the beast had large teeth, ears and beard and a head like a lion.

1727

Provincetown became incorporated and the petition was granted on June 14, 1727. The land was retained by the Province of Massachusetts Bay.

1741

The extreme tip of Cape Cod known as the Province Lands became a precinct of the Province of the Massachusetts Bay.

1746

The oldest, still-standing house in Provincetown, known as the Seth Nickerson house, was built at 72 Commercial Street.

1748

The English frigate *Somerset* was built in Chatham, England and launched carrying 64 guns.

1763

The first meeting house was built in Provincetown near the extreme northwest area known as "Old Cemetery."

1774

The *Somerset* which met its demise off the shore of Provincetown headed to the Americas.

1775

The American Revolution begins and Provincetown Harbor became the home base of operations for the British Royal Navy until 1783.

1776

Two vessels loaded with British provisions wreck offshore Provincetown and Truro and the goods recovered on the beaches by the locals are sent to aid George Washington's troops.

1778

The British frigate *Somerset* sank off Provincetown's Peaked Hill Bars and the wreck surfaced in North Truro. The bones, or wooden ribs of the *Somerset* have been exposed on occasion over the centuries by shifting sands and tides.

1783

The American Revolution officially ends on April 19.

1790

Provincetown's fishing fleets consists of twenty vessels.

1794

The town's first Methodist church was constructed on the corner of Bradford and Ryder Streets.

1795

Provincetown's first Masonic charter was signed by Paul Revere on December 12, 1795.

1797

The first lighthouse, the Highland Light, was built. Others following included Race Point in 1816, Long Point in 1826, and Wood End in 1873.

1798

Pease's Tavern was built this year next to the Customs House operated by Abner Dunham. It is now known as the Atlantic House on Masonic Place. Daniel Pease, Provincetown's first postmaster, was appointed in 1799.

1801

During the fall, smallpox became problematic and precautions were voted for at a special town meeting.

1802

Three ships from East India wrecked. The name of the ships were *Volusia*, *Ulysses* and *Brutus*. The crew of *Brutus* reached shore but all on board froze to death.

1807

Captain Stephen Nickerson, said to be one of the wealthiest men in Provincetown, opened his home at 54 Commercial Street as one of four houses in Provincetown functioning as part of the Underground Railroad during the Civil War.

1809

The war of 1812, preceded by the embargo of 1808, was also a time of disaster and great depression for Provincetown's fishermen.

1811

After the declaration of war with Britain, armed vessels surrounded Cape Cod with HMS. *Majestic* making her base at anchor between Provincetown and Truro.

1812

The fishing industry blossoms in Provincetown during the War of 1812.

1816

Race Point lighthouse was built to assist in the onslaught of maritime disasters.

1818

The first house was built on Long Point by John Atwood. Prince Freeman built the second house and Eldridge Smith the third. Long Point grew to a population of thirty-eight families and close to 200 adults who fished and manufactured salt.

1819

During the depression before the War of 1812, there was only one horse in Provincetown and it was a local legend because it was white and only had one eye.

1828

Six school districts were established in Provincetown, which led to creation of six schoolhouses.

1830

Long Point's first school was in the lighthouse. Three students were taught by Miss Sanborn.

1836

Provincetown's first fire engine, "Old Washington," was purchased.

1845

The town voted to petition the legislature to authorize the county commissioners to erect a jail at Provincetown near Central and Bradford Streets.

1850

Starting in 1850, families mysteriously began to move off of Long Point. Deacon John Dyer specialized in floating the buildings and moved most of the houses across Provincetown Harbor.

1852

Railroad was built in Provincetown and was incorporated as the Union Marine Railway.

1854

Windmills and ships dominated Provincetown's waterfront. Salt makers kept the windmills pumping the water into drying pans for the much-needed salt used to supply the fishing industry.

1858

Fire destroys six buildings on Commercial Street.

1864

Civil War batteries were constructed at Long Point under the charge of John Rosenthal for 12 years. Townspeople referred to the fortification as "Fort Useless" and "Fort Ridiculous."

1869

Provincetown's newspaper, the *Advocate*, was established.

1870

Bennett's Ice Plant began a lucrative business by cutting and storing 40 tons, building himself an icehouse and stable.

1871

The railroad was extended to Provincetown.

1872

In response to the huge amount of fatalities from maritime disasters off the Atlantic coast from 1870 to 1872, the US Lifesaving Service formed.

1873

Bradford Street, hastened by the opening of the railroad, was designed and created.

1875

Adams Hall, a large building at the corner of Winthrop and Commercial streets, caught on fire during the evening of March 4.

1877

Town hall on High Pole Hill burned down and the cause of the fire is still unknown. The site is the current location of the Pilgrim Monument.

1866

Work on Provincetown's present-day town hall, which is rumored to be haunted, started Sept. 10, 1885 and the building was dedicated in 1886.

1886

A six-eyed, slithering sea monster was reportedly spotted in Provincetown Harbor. Also, the Puritan shirt factory, owned by E. A. Buffinton of Leominster, was completely destroyed by fire.

1906

A bill was passed by Congress, and signed by President Theodore Roosevelt, to provide $40,000 from the Treasury of the US for the building of the Pilgrim Monument.

1907

Rose Dorothea wins the Lipton Cup and it's displayed in town hall.

1911

West End breakwater is constructed by the federal government to protect Provincetown Harbor from sand buildup.

1914

Mary Heaton Vorse's old house became home to the first Provincetown Players Theater welcoming artists like Eugene O'Neill and Tennessee Williams. During this era, the Bohemian lifestyle started to take root during the summer.

1917

Eugene O'Neill wrote *Ile*, a one-act play about "sail away lady" Viola Cook, wife of Captain John A. Cook of Provincetown. A Masonic Lodge member, Reuben Kelly, arrested two "spies" at gunpoint in the dining room of the Atlantic House Hotel. O'Neill was one of the men accused of spying.

1918

The flu epidemic that spread throughout the battlefields of Europe over to the US in 1918 also found its way to Provincetown.

1925

Provincetown Inn located at the beginning of Commercial Street is built.

1938

Tidal wave and hurricane unleashed disaster on the East Coast of the US. The hurricane impacted a massive area between Rhode Island and Provincetown.

1948

Father Silvia, of St. Peter's Catholic Church, was instrumental in the establishment of the "Blessing of the Fleet," along with Arthur Bragg Silva.

1969

Tony "Chop Chop" Costa was arraigned on charges of murder for three deaths on June 12, 1969. In May 1970, he was convicted of the murders of Mary Ann Wysocki and Patricia Walsh and sentenced to life in prison. Four years after his incarceration, Costa committed suicide by hanging himself in his cell.

1974

On July 26, 1974, the body of an unidentified white female was found in the dunes, approximately one mile east of Race Point Beach. She's known as the Lady of the Dunes.

1990

The 209-year-old Pilgrim House Hotel was destroyed in a midnight fire, burning the oldest hotel in Provincetown completely to the ground.

1991

The storm known as The Perfect Storm wallops Provincetown.

1996

Linda Silva, a long-time resident of Provincetown, was murdered on September 12, with a single shot to the head as she entered her car in the Alden Street parking lot.

2010

The allegedly haunted town hall reopens after renovations. Provincetown celebrates the 100-year anniversary of the dedication of the Pilgrim Monument.

The spot behind the Provincetown Inn is where the Pilgrims first set foot on Cape Cod four centuries ago. *Photo by Sam Baltrusis.*

SELECTED BIBLIOGRAPHY

The material in this book is drawn from published sources, including issues of *Boston Spirit, Provincetown Magazine, Provincetown Banner, Provincetown Advocate, Boston Globe, Boston Herald, Barnstable Patriot, The New York Times* and television programs, like *Unsolved Mysteries* and Syfy's *Ghost Hunters.* (For more information, refer to the text within the book.) Several books on Provincetown's paranormal history were used and cited throughout the text. Other New England–based websites and periodicals, like my various newspaper and magazine articles on the paranormal, Joni Mayhan's work for *Ghost Diaries,* Peter Muise's blog *New England Folklore, Provincetown Paranormal Research Society's* Facebook page, *Cape Cod Online,* Althea Boxell's files from the Provincetown History Preservation Project, websites from various local businesses and *Building Provincetown,* served as primary sources. I also conducted firsthand interviews, and some of the material is drawn from my own research. The Provincetown-based ghost tour, Haunted Ptown, was also a major source and generated original content. It should be noted that ghost stories are subjective, and I have made a concerted effort to stick to the historical facts, even if it resulted in debunking an alleged encounter with the paranormal.

Baltrusis, Sam. *Ghosts of Boston: Haunts of the Hub.* Charleston, SC: The History Press, 2012.

Baltrusis, Sam. *Ghosts of Cambridge: Haunts of Harvard Square and Beyond.* Charleston, SC: The History Press, 2013.

Baltrusis, Sam. *Ghosts of Salem: Haunts of the Witch City.* Charleston, SC: The History Press, 2014.

Balzano, Christopher. *Haunted Objects: Stories of Ghost on Your Shelf.* Iola, WI: Krause Publications, 2012.

Coogan, Jim. *Sail Away Ladies.* East Dennis, MA: Harvest Home Books, 2003.

D'Agostino, Thomas. *A Guide to Haunted New England.* Charleston, SC: The History Press, 2009.

Forest, Christopher. *North Shore Spirits of Massachusetts.* Atglen, PA: Schiffer Publishing, 2003.

Gellerman, Bruce and Sherman, Erik. *Massachusetts Curiosities.* Guilford, CT: The Globe Pequot Press, 2005.

Gordon, Dan and Joseph, Gary. *Cape Encounters: Contemporary Cape Cod Ghost Stories.* Hyannis, MA: Cockle Cove Press, 2004.

Hall, Thomas. *Shipwrecks of Massachusetts Bay.* Charleston, SC: The History Press, 2012.

Hauk, Dennis William. *Haunted Places: The National Directory*. New York: Penguin Group, 1996.

Jasper, Mark. *Haunted Cape Cod & The Islands*. Yarmouthport, MA: On Cape Publications, 2002.

Jasper, Mark. *Haunted Inns of New England*. Yarmouthport, MA: On Cape Publications, 2000.

Lawless, Debra. *Provincetown Since World War II: Carnival at Land's End*. Charleston, SC: The History Press, 2014.

Miller, Stauffer. *Cape Cod and the Civil War*. Charleston, SC: The History Press, 2010.

Muise, Peter. *Legends and Lore of the North Shore*. Charleston, SC: The History Press, 2014.

Nadler, Holly Mascott. *Ghosts of Boston Town: Three Centuries of True Hauntings*. Camden, ME: Down East Books, 2002.

Ogden, Tom. *The Complete Idiot's Guide to Ghosts & Hauntings*. Indianapolis, IN: Alpha Books, 2004.

Revai, Cheri. *Haunted Massachusetts: Ghosts and Strange Phenomena of the Bay State*. Mechanicsburg, PA: Stackpole Books, 2005.

Summers, Ken. *Queer Hauntings: True Tales of Gay & Lesbian Ghosts*. Mapleshade, NJ: Lethe Press, 2009.

Vorse, Mary Heaton. *Time and the Town: A Provincetown Chronicle*. New York, NY: Dial Press, 1942.

Zwicker, Roxie J. *Haunted Pubs of New England: Raising Spirits of the Past*. Charleston, SC: The History Press, 2007.